NEW ZEALAND SURFING GUIDE

• • • • • • • • • • • • • • • • • ▶

MIKE BHANA

NEW ZEALAND SURFING GUIDE

....................▶

MIKE BHANA

REED

Published by Reed Books, a division of Reed Publishing (NZ) Ltd, 39 Rawene Rd, Birkenhead, Auckland. Associated companies, branches and representatives throughout the world.

ISBN 0 7900 0492 5

First published 1988
Revised edition 1996

Printed in New Zealand

CONTENTS

INTRODUCTION

Surfing is one of the most exhilarating sports we can attempt. It is also one of the hardest to learn. Its origins stretch back to the royalty of the Hawaiian Islands.

New Zealand as a nation has historically turned towards the sea for its leisure activity. With the proximity of the main population centres to the coast and the fact that our main annual holiday break falls in the summer, it is only natural that Kiwis should be at home in the waves.

Surfing and riding the waves has been a favourite pastime for many Kiwis for more than two decades. Yet the acceptance of surfing as a sport, and recognition for the major growth industry that it has become, has only evolved during the past few years.

New Zealand is one huge playground for surfers. Its coasts are consistently pounded by swells from every angle and those prepared to travel for waves can be assured of finding surf almost every day of the year. The weather is mild to tropical in the north, mild to cold in the south of the South Island. Surfers can endure the water with a limited range of wetsuits (one spring suit and one good steamer and booties will do the trick) and still surf some of the best waves in the world.

New Zealand is one of the last large areas of surf and scenic coast yet to be exploited as a major surfing/tourist location. The locations that are listed within the pages of this book are just a few of the thousands of surf breaks that our coastline has to offer. There are still plenty of deserted and unknown breaks for those with a yearning for adventure.

New Zealand Surfing Guide is a collection of the most consistent, accessible and quality breaks in New Zealand. The information on breaks listed is a *guide only*, as weather conditions, surf, beach shape and the associated profile of a surfing location can vary. The author would therefore gratefully accept any information that challenges the material published in this book or on other breaks not included in this edition for possible future editions.

The book is broken into chapters addressing surf locations beginning in the north of the North Island and progressing south. Each chapter contains local information, history and amenities available should you be planning to stop over, and a breakdown of the area's key surf breaks.

At the back of the book is an index of surf breaks and surf spots to help in the location of particular areas you wish to visit.

If you are travelling for an extended period, this book can be used in association with a New Zealand road map. Detailed and relatively cheap maps are available through the Automobile Association. These maps are free to AA members, and the price of a complete set of maps, camping and accommodation guides and use of their many other services makes it worthwhile joining.

①.NORTHLAND

Northland is known as 'the winterless north' and has some of the most varied surfing locations set amongst some of the country's most scenic coastal areas. From Cape Reinga in the Far North the surf begins. Places like Tapotupotu Bay and Spirits Bay have good waves in a northerly swell. South to the white east coast sands of Parengarenga Harbour mouth and on down the east coast, the waves abound. The reefs and beaches from Cape Karikari down to Bream Head have some great waves and certainly the warmest and clearest waters in the country.

On the west coast there is the famous Ninety Mile Beach with good surf at the northern end (Scott Point — best in a small swell), the Bluff and, at its southern end, one of the country's premier left-hand points, Shipwreck Bay. The west coast from Shipwreck Bay south to Baylys Beach remains relatively unexplored surf country and many surfers know of secret breaks hidden by the farmland and forest that are as good as any in the country, but getting to them is often more trouble than it is worth. If you are planning to check out any unknown areas for surf, make sure you let someone know where you are planning to go and for how long; if you have to cross farmland, get the farmer's permission.

Northland's coasts offer the travelling surfer a lot more than just surfing. The northern waters are rich in game fish and offer some of the country's finest diving locations — places like the Poor Knights Islands, the Hen and Chickens, the Bay of Islands and the Cavalli Islands, home of the wreck of the *Rainbow Warrior*. The inshore waters have good safe anchorage, good fishing and shellfish.

The best time of year to plan a trip here is during the summer and autumn, December through to April, when there is swell on the west coast and often

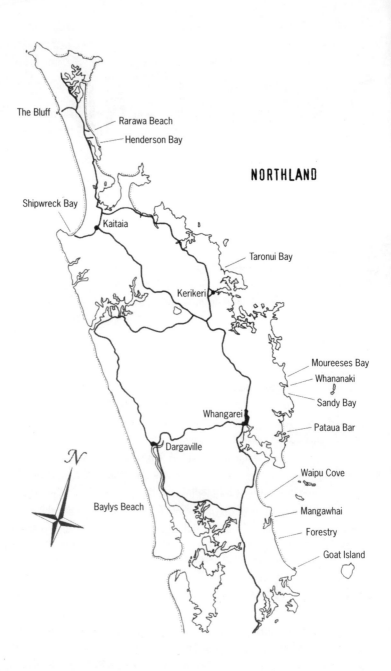

The Bluff

Rarawa Beach

Henderson Bay

NORTHLAND

Shipwreck Bay

Kaitaia

Taronui Bay

Kerikeri

Moureeses Bay

Whananaki

Sandy Bay

Whangarei

Pataua Bar

Dargaville

Waipu Cove

Baylys Beach

Mangawhai

Forestry

Goat Island

N

good cyclone swells or north-east swells on the east coast. Surfing good waves at Shipwreck requires a special trip and the surf cannot be easily predicted. It needs a good 4- to 5-m swell to break properly, and it is the only place to surf on the North Island's west coast should the swell get this big or bigger.

The surf breaks listed are a guide to some of the better and/or more consistent breaks in Northland and are only a few of the many breaks that pepper these coasts.

THE BLUFF

A rocky outcrop 66 km north on Ninety Mile Beach, the Bluff is accessible from Te Kao on SH1 or by driving up along the beach at low tide. Known to the Maori as Te Wakatehaua, the surrounding land is owned by the local Maori community and permission must be gained to camp. The Bluff offers good fishing and Ninety Mile Beach has plenty of shellfish. Watch the incoming tide if you're driving on the beach as there is no good inland access at the Bluff, only a deep soft sand track to the road. The nearest garage and shop is at Te Kao, so when you intend to stay bring everything you'll need with you. Fires are a no-no as the Aupouri State Forest lies just behind the dunes.

The Bluff has some excellent beach breaks on the south side, but often the best waves are to be had on the north side in a south swell on the incoming tide. Swell from the south-west drives straight in and when Shipwreck is flat there are often good waves to be had here. It is best in a 1.2- to 1.8-m south to south-west swell on the north side and in a north-west swell on the south side. Offshores blow from the north to the south-east, and the best time to surf it is from mid to high tide. Entry is easiest from the rocks out on the Bluff; watch the rips that take you out and down the beach. Surfers should also beware of the vicious sandflies and mosquitoes that run rampant here. As Bluff is the only reef for miles of sandy beach, this spot is notorious for sharks too. Good luck!

RARAWA BEACH

Rarawa Beach is one of Northland's most beautiful. It lies at the southern tip of Great Exhibition Bay on the east coast and access is from SH1 north of Ngataki. Rarawa has an excellent camping ground beside the Ngataki River that flows into Great Exhibition Bay at the south end of the beach. The pure white silica sands of this region are the primary source of silica for New Zealand's glass industry. The beach is about 2 km long, the rocky headland to the north separating the beach from Great Exhibition Bay. Because of the glare factor of the linen-white sands and the clarity of the water, the sun can have a double burning effect. Through the summer and during the months of spring and autumn surfers should take extra precautions to combat the sun's added strength.

Rarawa faces north and catches swell from the east through to the north. It can be surfed on all tides but is better on half to full in swells from 0.6 to 1.8 m. Offshore winds blow from west to south. The beach's sandbanks vary with the seasons and are often best during the months of January through to April. When the banks are good this beach can provide excellent hollow waves set amongst some of New Zealand's best scenery.

HENDERSON BAY

Hendersons is on the east coast about 40 km north of Kaitaia. The road is well signposted and is between the settlements of Waihopo and Ngataki. One of the main attractions of beaches around this piece of the east coast is the white silica sand. The beach stretches from the road's end south to Grenville Point. The area offers good fishing and diving around the reefs to the north. There is a backpackers' a few hundred metres from the beach, with the next nearest accommodation either at Houhora to the south or Rarawa Beach camping ground to the north. Houhora has accommodation, shops, petrol and a hotel.

The best surfing at Hendersons can be found at the northern end of the beach below the road's end. This part of the beach faces to the north-east and is best surfed in north-westerly to south-westerly winds. The beach features a series of reefs that together with sandbanks can create some excellent waves. It is best in 1 to 2 m from north-east or east although swell from the north can get into the bay. Best tide is from mid to high, although the reefs and beach sandbars are almost always surfable during good swells.

SHIPWRECK BAY

The title 'winterless north' applies especially to this sheltered part of New

Zealand. Shipwreck Bay, or Ahipara Bay, lies at the southernmost tip of Ninety Mile Beach and borders the coastal township of Ahipara, which is about 14 km west of New Zealand's northernmost town of Kaitaia. The name Kaitaia is Maori for 'abundance of food' and the coasts around the town are rich in seafood. Kaitaia offers an extensive range of tourist excursions including bus trips along Ninety Mile Beach and a tour right around the surf breaks of Shipwreck.

Ahipara was a gumdigging area during its early history. Today it is a retreat for summer holidaymakers who come here to sample the sunshine and seafood. A word of warning to surfers intending to soak up the sun here: it gets really hot in the summer, especially if you're walking for waves, and if the heat doesn't get you the burn factor from glare in the water will cook you to a crisp. The township has a store, a gas station and a good camping ground, while back in Kaitaia there are all the facilities that could possibly be needed, including a youth hostel and several backpackers' for cheaper-than-cheap accommodation.

Shipwreck Bay is probably one the country's best set-ups, but it requires very big swells to rap into the multitude of left-hand breaks. Arriving at the bay, access to the breaks is by foot, four-wheel-drive or a rugged and sometimes risky drive around the rocks by car. The bay itself faces almost due north and is the start of the headland called **Point** or **Tauroa Point**. The further you travel around the rocks the more westerly the outlook, until it finally joins the west coast. The rip runs around the point and in towards Shipwreck Bay. Surfers can return from breaks further west by riding the rip between the breaks, walking the bigger gaps and surfing through the changing line-ups. Shipwreck Bay is the inside break of a chain of breaks and for it to be ridable here a forecast of at least 5 m from the south-west or 4 m from the west is needed.

Peaks is the first break you come to as you head around the reef about 1 km west. It begins at the end of the rock shelf that stretches from the bay and is best in swell anywhere from 4 to 7 m — providing waves to the break of about 1 to 2 m. Best time of the tide is low incoming, and a good swell and the right sand can produce fast peeling waves from Peaks right through into Shipwreck Bay, producing up to three-minute rides. Offshore winds along the reef are south-west to south-east, and Shipwreck Bay can offer ridable waves even in westerly winds. Entry can be made at any point along the reef or from the bay inside the take-off reef at Peaks. The wave begins over a shallow reef and then fires off along the edge of the rocky shelf across a sand bottom. The first part of the wave is hollow and can provide a good tube, the wave then heads off down the rocks and can have some exciting sections depending on the sand. The higher the tide, the bigger the swell needs to be for it to break.

Almost 1 km further west from Peaks is **Mukerau 1** or **Mukie 1**, in a small bay before the reefs begin heading west again. Mukie 1 is another left-hand break over sand and is generally smaller than Peaks or waves at the other breaks further west. It requires good sand buildup and can produce a fast barrelling wave that can peel for over 50 m. It is offshore in winds from east through to south-west and is best from 0.6 to 1.8 m on any tide, but it favours high tide. Entry is best made from the bay out along the line-up.

Next is **Mukerau II** or **Mukie II**. It breaks from outside the next bay, past a little headland parallel to the take-off at Mukie 1. Mukie II is bigger than the previous breaks and faces a little more to the west. It is best surfed on high or in smaller swells on a lower tide. It breaks from 1.2 to 2.4 m over sand that builds up along the reef. The take-off can be quite heavy and square. It can produce a good top-to-bottom wave and deep tubes. Offshore is south-east to south-west and Mukie II is best on a west to south-west swell.

Outside Mukie II is **Supertubes**, a fast section filled wave that breaks over a combination of shallow sharp reef and sand. It is best in waves from 1.5 to 3 m. When it's big enough to break it will work on all tides, with the best tide being low incoming. The take-off can be as difficult as you make it, as a shallow reef lies across the take-off zone. The first section can produce some excellent tubes, especially in a larger swell. The wave then peels off for several hundred metres to eventually join up with Mukie II and on, if you're lucky, to join Mukie I, making a ride over a kilometre long. Entry is from either outside Mukie II or from the bay between Supertubes and Pines and then across outside the take-off area.

Pines is easily identified by the pine trees that extend down the hill in front of the break. Pines is best in a smaller swell, from 1 to 1.5 m at high tide. It breaks both left and right on the smaller swells over a sand and shallow reef bottom. Entry is best out through one of the many sandy gaps in the reefs and isn't too hard. Offshore winds blow from the south to east and the break faces to the west-north-west.

A good 4 km from Shipwreck Bay is the last notable surf break before the west coast. Called **Blue House**, it was named after the farmhouse it breaks in front of. Though the house has long since changed colour, it is the only one around this part of the coast so the spot is easy to find. The break begins a little west of the farmhouse and peels for a hundred metres or more down the reef heading east. It is always much bigger here than any of the other breaks as the waves don't have to wrap around the reef so far to get in. It is also the most dangerous of the breaks, peeling over shallow, sharp, barnacle-encrusted reef. It breaks best at high tide in 1.2- to 2.4-m waves. Getting in and out is extremely difficult, especially on big swells. Negotiating the shallow, barnacle-encrusted reef to get out almost always ends in a few cuts and scrapes to both rider and board. If you are not sure, don't go out. The wave starts fast, backs off, and then rifles off again over a razor-sharp and very shallow ledge. It can produce very heavy and deep barrels. If you get nailed, keep your head up. Offshore winds are south-easterlies or light southerlies.

TARONUI BAY

Taronui Bay lies about 15 km north of Kerikeri township, the nearest centre for accommodation, provisions and garages. Access is via a farm road through private property and there is often a gate charge during the summer to get down the road. It is also known by the name of the creek that flows into the bay, Tapuaetahi. The bay contains several surf breaks on the offshore reefs and rugged points.

Tapuaetahi has a reef in the centre of a calm sandy bay. The reef draws the swell onto its shallows, leaving the beach relatively calm for easy entry. The reef breaks both left and right, the left being best on low tide while the right is best surfed on mid to high tide. Tapuaetahi needs a large swell as the bay is protected by an outer reef and is relatively sheltered from the easterly swells by its northerly outlook. A 2- to 3-m swell from the north or the north-east offers the best 1.2- to 2.4-m conditions, and offshore winds are from the south-west to south-east quarter. Paddling out from the beach is fairly easy but the waves on the reef can be very heavy, breaking over very shallow reef. Both the left and the right can provide good tubes in a clean swell but if you're caught inside on a lower tide, the trip over the reef can be a nerve-racking experience. The reef breaks whenever there is a big clean swell and in larger swells the left point at the western end of the bay can provide good rides and some pretty insane tubes when the sand is adequately built up against the rock shelf, but it rarely breaks with any form.

Elliots is a right-hand point five minutes' walk west of Tapuaetahi, across the river around the inside of the lagoon, over the lupin bank, around a small boulder bay and then over and down a steep rock shelf. When the reef at Tapuaetahi is 2.4 m, Elliots is a solid 1.8 m. The point can be surfed from 1 to 2.4 m, faces north and is offshore in similar winds to the reef at Tapuaetahi. It also picks up similar swell and the sand on the point is good for most of the year. At mid to high tide the break is best as it draws more of the swell and the shallow boulders on the inside have plenty of water covering them. As the tide gets lower the take-off can get fairly exciting and produce a good barrel section over the shallow boulders and reef. Elliots is also known for the odd shark sighting. Entry is off the rock wall that the waves break down and a good jump can put the surfer straight into the line-up.

Around the headland to the east of Tapuaetahi is a break aptly named **The Ledge**. It is as heavy as the east coast gets and doesn't start to break until the swell is 1.8 to 2.4 m. The bigger the swell the better, and it is best surfed on low tide. Don't surf here or even go out if you aren't a good surfer or don't have at least a 2-m reef board. The wave is a barrel from start to finish and the reef is knee-deep below. There is no flat or easy take-off; it is a hardcore wave for the hardcore only.

MOUREESES

Moureeses Bay is a quiet little sheltered beach that can be reached by following the road to Whananaki North, then on out to the end of the holiday resort, following the road north over the hill to Tauwhara Bay and on over the next hill to Moureeses. The bay has no facilities at all and the nearest toilets, provisions and petrol are back at Whananaki.

The beach is broken into two smaller bays by a small reef, and the best waves are often at the southern end of the southern part of the bay. Here there is often a good bank off the reef that can produce an excellent little right-hander that peels over the shallow sandbar to the beach. Moureeses is best in small swells, but the swell here is often smaller than the rest of the coast because of the reefs and islands that protect the ends of the bay. When the swell in open water is about 1.5 to 2 m from the north-east or east, then the best 0.6- to 1.2-m conditions can be encountered here. The banks can be surfed on any tide, the best conditions being on the low incoming tide on smaller swells or mid to high on a bigger swell. The waves are soft and forgiving but fast and can produce a fun little tube. There is a camping ground if you wish to stay, but bring everything you will need including cooking equipment. Offshore winds blow from the south-west or west although the bay remains reasonably protected in winds from the south or north.

WHANANAKI

Whananaki North is a small seaside holiday resort about 42 km north-east of Whangarei. Best access is through Hikurangi out through Marua Rd and on to Whananaki South Rd, then take Haile Rd to join up with Whananaki North Rd. The town is set on the banks of the Whananaki Inlet and there is a shop, petrol and camping accommodation here. The Inlet offers safe anchorage and good cockle beds, while the mouth of the inlet produces some good waves and reasonable fishing.

The bar is a left-hander that is fast and best surfed on a low incoming tide in an east or south-east swell. Because the bar faces to the south, the swell needs to be reasonably big to have enough power to wrap around the headland and get in to break over the sandbar. Swell from 1.2 to 1.8 m offers the best waves and the best entry is from the inlet by either paddling across to the sandy spit and going out through the shore break, or by going out through the channel and paddling across into the take-off zone from the north. The best winds for surfing here are either north-westerlies or light northerlies. The beach to the south also has good waves on the shifting banks. The best place to check out is the far southern end where there is ofte. a good right-hand bank. Access to the beach is by foot only.

SANDY BAY

Sandy Bay is one of the most surfed beaches in this area and is the main beach for surfers from the Whangarei area. The best access is via Hikurangi. Marua Rd and then Matapouri Rd will take you straight into the bay. From the bay the Poor Knights Islands can easily be seen about 25 km to the north-east and the road continues around to the south to Tutukaka Harbour, the base for charter boats that take divers out to the island marine reserve for some of the best and most scenic diving in the country. The port is also one of the major bases for Northland's game fishing industry. Between the Bay of Islands and Tutukaka some of the world's game fishing records have been broken and set over the years.

Sandy Bay is recognised as a good surfing bay and local competitions are often held here, but don't hold out too much hope for the quality of the surf. It is a steep-profiled bay that faces to the north-east and produces a series of sandbanks that wander around the bay through the seasons. The waves are short and snappy and the boards that locals surf here indicate the type of waves they get and surf. The best wave is often a right-hander at the south-eastern end of the bay. The best swell is a north-easterly about 0.6 to 1.5 m in winds from the south-west. The best tide is incoming, though the bay has waves on all tides. There are also reasonable waves to be had in the bays to the north, though getting to them requires walking.

PATAUA BAR

Pataua Bar is accessible from either Pataua or Pataua North, with the best access from Pataua North. From Kamo or Whangarei head out on the road past the Whangarei Falls towards Tutukaka. Turn left into Harris Rd and then left into Wherora Rd. This will link you up with the Pataua North Rd.

The bar lies at the southern end of Ngunguru Bay at the mouth of the Pataua River and is a fast-breaking and hollow right-hander. It is best in swell from the north-east or east and from 1 to 1.8 m. The waves break across the shallow sandbar best on the low to mid incoming tide, but the bigger the swell the better the surf is on the higher tide. The waves are hollow and often unmakable, but the barrels are worth the trip. The best winds blow from the south-west and access is via the rivermouth on the outgoing or dead tide. The waves here are often like those of Whangapoua on Great Barrier Island and their form depends a lot on the shape of the bar. The best time of year to check it out is from December through to April. Because of the isolation of this break, make sure of the conditions before venturing out here. If you travel out and the waves are no good, it is a long trip to the next good break to the north. There are also good beach breaks to be had on smaller swells up and down the length of Ngunguru Bay. The banks vary from swell to swell but there is almost always a good right and left peak to be had on the mid to high tide.

BAYLYS BEACH

Baylys is a long black-sand beach that runs along the west coast from North Head, at the mouth of the Kaipara Harbour, north to Maunganui Bluff. The beach and the sand dunes that lie beneath the pasture inland make up part of the huge sandbar built up at the mouth of the Kaipara over the centuries. Within these consolidated sand dunes lie a series of lakes, the most well known being the Kai Iwi Lakes about 30 km north of Dargaville. They lie within the Taharoa Domain and offer good camping, trout fishing and sailing.

Baylys Beach is a well-known fishing beach that is well used by the people of Dargaville. It is about 12 km west of Dargaville on Baylys Coast Rd. There are camping facilities at the beach, but for any provisions or petrol a trip back to Dargaville is required.

The surf here is best on small swells from any westerly direction. The beach faces to the west and is offshore in any winds from the easterly quarter. The best swell size is from 0.6 to 1.2 m and the best tide is incoming mid to high. If the swell is much bigger the beach gets very messy and dangerous. The sandbars around the road's end often form up as good as anywhere on the beach, but there are also good waves to be had north at Maunganui Bluff. Again the swell needs to be small. On the high tide the banks here can form good right- and left-hand peaks that are hollow and fast.

WAIPU COVE

Waipu Cove is the small seaside resort that lies in the southernmost corner of Bream Bay. It is a short drive some 8 km east of Waipu, and has good motor camp accommodation with cabins and tent and caravan sites. The township of Waipu just off SH1 has all the necessities, including takeaways and a pub.

The town of Waipu has a Scottish history and was founded by Norman McLeod in 1853 when he and about 120 fellow Scots Highlanders moved on from Nova Scotia in Canada to settle here. Not long after their arrival in New Zealand news of their settlement reached Nova Scotia and a further 850 or so Highlanders migrated from Canada to join the settlement in Waipu.

From the Cove surfers can see Marsden Pt at the northern end of Bream Bay and north-east in the bay lie the Hen and Chicken Islands. Inland and about 12 km to the north on the Waipu Caves Rd lie the Waipu Limestone Caves. The Cove itself is part of the final curve of Bream Bay before a rocky headland separates it from the other beaches to the south.

Waipu Cove is best surfed in a small swell from 0.6 to 1.5 m from the east or north-east. It faces to the north-east and is offshore in south-westerlies or westerlies. The waves break off a rocky headland or on a series of bars to the north up the beach. The bars are fickle and move about with each new swell, although there is almost always a bank that is working in a small swell. The beach can be surfed on any tide but the best waves can often be found on an incoming tide when they have a little extra push.

To the south is **Langs Beach** which also has some reasonable beach breaks, especially on a smaller swell. The banks here are not as reliable as Waipu, but when they are in good shape the beach can provide some good waves. Access is by road to the south and the bay faces east to pick up the same swell as Waipu.

MANGAWHAI HEADS

Mangawhai Heads is about 10 km north of Mangawhai township. It is named Mangawhai because of the abundance of stingrays. The Mangawhai River flows into a salty harbour estuary before flowing into the sea on the south side of the heads. There is accommodation, petrol, food and other provisions to be found in the township. Getting to the heads, surfers can come through the hills from Waipu Cove 12 km to the north-west or inland from Kaiwaka on SH1.

The surf can be divided into two main areas — the bar to the south and the beach below the surf club on the northern side of the Mangawhai River.

Mangawhai Beach is best in swells from 0.6 to 1.8 m and depends on the banks. It faces to the east and is best on a mid to high tide. Offshores blow from the west to south.

Mangawhai Bar is a left-hander that peels across the rivermouth over a sand bottom. This used to be the entrance to the harbour, but sand build-up has made it unworkable and the entry is now well south. It is best surfed on the low to incoming tide and the bar can handle 1.2- to 2-m swells from the north-east to east. Offshores are from the west to south-west with north-westerlies adding a nasty cross-chop.

FORESTRY

Forestry, as the name implies, is accessible through state forest. It is on the east coast about 24 km to the north-east of Wellsford. It lies on the south side of Te Arai Pt and is at the top of Pakiri Beach. The forestry area directly inland is dotted with a series of small lakes. The last few kilometres of road are only open during the hours of daylight, but there is a camping area north of Te Arai

Pt at Black Swamp. Food, petrol and so on are available back at Wellsford and surfers should bring everything they need with them. Getting to Forestry requires a tricky piece of navigation and travellers intending to head out to surf here are best advised to get a good map or follow other surfers as they negotiate the dusty backroads.

Forestry Beach faces to the east and sits in the lee of Te Arai Pt. The bay is best in small swells, 0.6 to 1.5 m from the east or north-east, and in winds from the south-west through to the north-west. The beach is best surfed on a mid to high incoming tide and once the tide turns to go out the form of the beach rapidly deteriorates. If the swell is on the smaller side the bay can be surfed on all tides. The bars vary through the seasons but there are usually a reasonable couple of banks for most of the year with a fairly regular left-hander peeling off from beside the point.

Te Arai Point, on the north side of the rocky headland, can also offer good waves, though the banks are more fickle than those to the south. Again the bay is best in small swells from the north-east to south-east but the beach is more exposed to winds from the northerly quarter. Best times to watch the banks are through the late summer months.

Both these breaks are known for shark sightings, and with the headland being the only reef for miles, the waters are rich in sea life.

GOAT ISLAND

Goat Island is a marine reserve that lies to the north of the township of Leigh. Leigh is the closest centre and has a pub, takeaway food, a grocery store and petrol. It is easily found by taking the turn-off on the north side of the town of Warkworth and heading north-east about 21 km.

Goat Island was New Zealand's first marine reserve and the 500 ha of water surrounding the island has full protection for the sea life that abounds here. This means strictly NO fishing. The waters may only be used for research and recreation. If you're planning to spend a few days here then bring your mask and snorkel because the tame and prolific fish life is a sight worth seeing. Hand feeding a 14-kg snapper is quite an experience.

When the seas are too heavy to venture in for a snorkel, the north-facing reefs offer excellent waves. They need a big 1.6 to 2.6-m swell, preferably from the north or north-east. The waves break right out in front of the carpark and peak up over the low reef to form a good solid right-hander that can wall up for 50 m, but the swell needs to be big to get in. A swell forecast of a solid 2 to 3 m should do the trick and if the wind is blowing from the south-west to south-east, and the tide is mid to high, then Goat Island can provide some good waves.

If the swell is up but the winds are blowing from the north or north-east, then there is a break to the south called **Daniels Reef**. It is best on a high tide in a big swell as the waves have to wrap around Cape Rodney to get in. Access is from just south of the township of Leigh; Wonderview Rd takes you to a walkway that leads down to the bay. Again the swell must be big to get in here. It is a right-hand break that breaks over a very shallow reef and can only be surfed an hour or so either side of high tide.

North of Goat Island is the start of **Pakiri Beach**, a long sandy beach that can have good waves in any easterly swell from 0.6 to 1.8 m. The beach faces to the east and is offshore in a westerly or south-westerly wind. The best access is via the road that travels north from Goat Island. The beach has a steep profile and is best around high tide. The waves are often short, hollow beach breaks that hit sandbars which change and move with each new swell. The best place is often straight out in front of the Pakiri Beach carpark, or just to the north at the rivermouth.

AUCKLAND

Auckland is New Zealand's largest city and consequently the area of the country with the highest population of surfers. The city lies on a narrow isthmus between two harbours, the Manukau and the Waitemata, which empty into the Tasman Sea and the Hauraki Gulf, on the east coast, respectively.

For Aucklanders this means a centrally based surfer can get to either west or east coast within a 40-minute drive. The only problem is that the east coast, which is within easy reach of Aucklanders, remains relatively protected by the islands of the Gulf, Great Barrier Island and the Coromandel Peninsula. There are some good east coast surf locations within the city's limits but the surf is rare, and when it is up it lasts only a short time. There are usually about five to ten storm surfs a year on the city beaches and a couple of north-easterly ground swells a year will be big enough to get into places like Long Bay Reef, Milford Reef, Takapuna Reef and the East Coast Bays beaches.

For the more serious surf animals there are a number of west coast surf beaches within 40 minutes' drive of the city. They stretch from Muriwai in the north down the craggy coastline bordered by the Waitakere Ranges to Whatipu on the northern side of the Manukau Heads. The beaches nestle amongst the cliffs and headlands and offer excellent waves all year round. The offshore winds blow from north-east to south-east and some places like Piha Bar are quite ridable in a southerly wind providing it is not too strong. There are two reform-type waves that can be ridden even in onshore days, but only on the full tide — one at Piha and one at O'Neills. Surfers should be wary of this stretch of coast, especially in big swells, as the rips and holes are notorious claimers of lives. You should also be wary of the summertime crowds that swarm over the beaches and the waves, sending fibreglass projectiles in all directions in the surf.

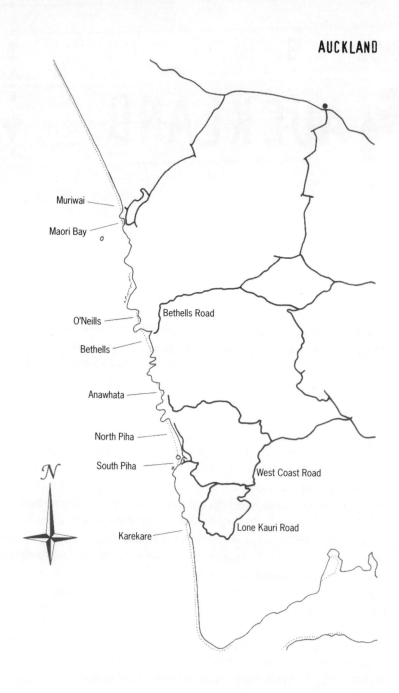

AUCKLAND

Muriwai

Maori Bay

Bethells Road

O'Neills

Bethells

Anawhata

North Piha

South Piha

West Coast Road

Lone Kauri Road

Karekare

𝒩

MURIWAI BEACH

Muriwai Beach is about 40 minutes from Auckland via SH16. Accommodation is available at the Muriwai camping ground. There is a petrol pump at the Muriwai Store, back up from the beach, along with a good range of food, provisions and surf wax.

The rock ledge to the south of the beach is a popular surfcasting spot and during easterlies the beach is often used by kite long-line fishers. Surfers should be wary of the kite lines as the nylon and hooks are hard to see and often appear head high in the surf when the lines are being pulled in.

Muriwai also boasts an excellent golf course and one of the top surf lifesaving clubs in the country.

Muriwai Beach is classified as a public road and at low tide the black sand can easily be driven on. Beware of the soft, drier sand around and above the high tide mark, and the incoming tide. Many unwary drivers have been caught by the advancing tides and the rusting roofs of these sunken victims lie trapped as a reminder to future travellers.

Department of Conservation workers continue to plant the dunes along Muriwai in marram grass in an attempt to stabilise the movement inland of the black sand. Respect their work and stay off the planted areas.

Muriwai Beach runs from the mouth of the Kaipara Harbour to the headland at Muriwai. There are good waves to be found all along it on the always changing banks. Muriwai is best on an incoming tide with clean swell from any direction. Best size is from 0.6 to 1.8 m. Best places are often just off the headland or about 1 km north at the rivermouth. The bar in the south corner is a left-hander and entry is either from the beach or off the rocks. Off the rocks entry drops the surfer straight into the rip that moves north and right through the line-up. This break favours the bigger 1.5- to 1.8-m size range.

During days of smaller waves good banks can be found at the rivermouth to the north and all along the coast up to Rimmers Rd. During the summer months Muriwai becomes very crowded. Surfers should avoid the flagged areas and be wary of swimmers, bodyboarders, clubbies, grommets and, most dangerous of all, goatboaters and jetskiers.

Rimmers Road is accessible from SH16 about 15 km north of the Muriwai turn-off. Rimmers Rd is a forestry access road and is closed to the public during the hours of darkness.

Rimmers is best when the forecast predicts no significant swell or up to 1 m.

Often when the waves at Muriwai or Maori Bay are too small to be ridden, Rimmers has good waves. Best size is from 0.6 to 1.2 m on a clean swell from any direction. However, Rimmers is easily affected by sea breezes and strong winds. The waves break on an array of banks, providing fast tubing rides. The best tide is mid incoming to high and the quality deteriorates rapidly as the tide begins to go out.

MAORI BAY

Maori Bay is on the west coast, just over the hill south of Muriwai. On reaching Muriwai, descend towards the beach to turn left up the hill just before the first speed bumps on the approach to the beach. The road is posted Maori Bay. A right turn halfway up the hill takes you into the carpark. Like the carparks at Muriwai, the gate to the Maori Bay carpark is locked at night and a signpost at the entrance will tell you when you have to get your car out before you end up staying the night.

Accommodation is available at the Muriwai camping ground in the form of tent and caravan sites, and cabins. Petrol is available at the Muriwai Store but the nearest garage facilities are back at Waimauku. The nearest pub is at Kumeu.

The area around the headland between Muriwai and Maori Bay is home to one of the area's few gannet colonies. Tracks from the north end of the Maori Bay carpark lead to lookouts over the colony and offer a good overview of both Maori Bay and Muriwai Beach. The island of Oaia, just offshore, provides sanctuary for nesting gannets and terns and also boasts a seal colony.

Maori Bay can be divided into three major surf areas. All are offshore in easterly winds, and high cliffs provide good protection from strong offshores. The bay is ridable in north-east to south-east winds but winds from northern and southern quarters are borderline. Access from the carpark is steep and rocky. Sharp stones and broken glass can be avoided by wearing jandals (thongs) down to the beach.

The beach has left- and right-hand banks on a sand bottom. It is best from mid to high on an incoming tide. The breaks can get quite punchy and hollow with the push of the tide although rides are usually short. Best size is from 1.2 to 1.8 m with a swell from the south-west quarter. Best viewing is from the carpark or the gannet viewing platforms. Entry is reasonably easy from mid beach but during larger swells enter further south to combat the north-travelling rip. The bigger the swell, the stronger the rip. There is no surf rescue at Maori Bay so if you get caught in the rip go with it around the headland, staying away from the rocks, and paddle in at Muriwai or raise your hand to alert the patrol on Muriwai Beach.

Shag Rock is a long left-hander at the south end of the beach. It is a fickle break and depends on the shifting sands. It is best from 1.2 to 2.4 m on a low incoming tide and the best time of year to watch for it is from August to January. Ten metres inside the rock is a ledge that can produce an interesting and critical take-off. A small rock visible at low tide and about 20 m further north can cause a section on larger swells.

Further south is **Mussel Rock**. It is predominantly a right-hander but also has a shorter left. It is usually bigger here than the other breaks in the bay and a lot heavier. Best from 1.2 to 2.4 m on a low incoming tide. The bottom is as the name suggests although good sand build-up outside the rock is essential to drag in the swell. Access is by paddle from the beach inside Shag Rock or by entry from the rocks inside the break. The paddle is easier, especially in larger swells. The wave has a heavy square take-off followed by a long wall and is not recommended for the inexperienced.

Being caught inside here during a good set will test the best duck-divers against a backdrop of high cliffs and rugged rocks. Best viewing is from the carpark.

Other breaks around Maori Bay include more peaks south of Shag Rock and a left-hand point at the far end of the next cove, but they break rarely and only in smaller swells. Access is very difficult, either at low tide or a paddle from the bay.

BETHELLS BEACH

Bethells Beach, or Te Henga, lies south of Maori Bay and is accessible through Swanson and Bethells Rd. The beach is another summer retreat for Aucklanders who flock to the west coast during the sunny season. It is about 45 km west of Auckland and has a surf patrol, good fishing from the rocks and good bush walks.

Bethells is a reasonable-sized beach and is best surfed on smaller swells from the north-west through to the south-west in the 0.6- to 1.5-m range. When the swell is bigger the beach tends to just close out and it can get quite rippy and dangerous. There are a couple of spots worth checking out — the middle of the beach (just south of the patrolled area) and behind Ihumoana Island at the northern end. The island often has a good, fast and hollow right-hander that breaks behind it and peels through to the bay on a low incoming tide. The breaks on the beach, however, are best on mid to high incoming tides. There is a medium to strong rip at either end of the beach on the bigger swell and in the middle between the banks where there is often a dangerous hole. When the tide turns to go out, these rips become quite strong and can get the inexperienced surfer into all sorts of trouble.

O'Neill Bay is a short walk over the sand dune and headland to the north of Bethells. The beach is much the same as Bethells, being best on smaller swells, but the southern corner of O'Neills has a high tide right-hand reform wave that is similar to The Ditch at Piha. It can provide some fun little waves.

PIHA

Thirty-five kilometres south-west of Auckland is Piha Beach. Piha's surfing history goes back to the very roots of surfing in New Zealand during the early sixties. Over the years it has come to be the most popular beach in New Zealand for several reasons: it is only 40 minutes from New Zealand's largest city, Auckland, and can offer consistently good waves in most conditions. Access from the city is easy via the western suburbs by car, bike or bus. The beach has an excellent camping ground, a shop, a takeaway bar and two surf clubs.

The beach is separated into north and south Piha by Lion Rock, a huge monolith of volcanic lava that bears a plaque commemorating those killed in the two world wars. An excellent but steep walk up the Lion takes you to a viewing platform that overlooks the coastline and all the breaks. Inland the area has some excellent bush walks and reasonable fishing can be had around both the north and south headlands and Lion Rock. During the summer months this beach is overrun with crowds from the city and its waves are some of the most crowded in the country. The two surf lifesaving clubs are among New Zealand's best, and with the number of rescues they are involved in over the summer it is not hard to see why. The beach faces due west and, like most of our west coast beaches, is prone to rips and holes, especially on the outgoing tide. If the swell is over 1.5 m, young surfers should be wary about paddling out the back of the waves if they are too far from the patrolled area. Piha is also notorious for the sheer volume of surf equipment present in the waves, including wave skis, malibu surfboards, bodyboards and patrol craft.

Starting at the south end of the beach is **The Bar**. It breaks often from outside Nun Rock and peels across the bay to form an excellent left-hander. If the sand is good the wave can barrel for over 50 metres. It will work on most tides, though it is best on low incoming. It needs a fairly big swell to break on high tide. The best winds blow from the south-east through to the north-east and the bar is surfable in southerlies if they are light. Best size is from 1.2 to 1.8 m, but if the sand is good the bar can handle over 2.4 m. In less than 2 m of swell the wave starts as a fast section across Submarine Rock and peels off a little flatter past the rock called the Beehive to fire off fast and hollow across the section in front of the rocks into the bay. The Bar is ridable for most of the year but the best time to check it out is summer through autumn and early winter. Entry can be straight out from the beach in smaller swells or from the Nun in bigger swells. To get to the Nun surfers must traverse the rocks at the south end of the bay around into the cove. You can then either take the rip out past the outside of the Beehive through the impact zone or head south of the Nun around the cove and venture out through the cave that goes through Nun Rock to enter the surf just inside Submarine Rock. This is definitely for the experienced and first timers should follow a local along this route.

For younger surfers, and for all when the winds are onshore, there is **The Ditch**. It works only on full tide and is a right-hander that peels from just outside the southern rocks into the southern corner of the bay. It works best in a big swell and is a soft reform wave that seldom has a face more than 1.2 m high, although for most of the people who surf here 1.2 m is over head height. It is here that many of Auckland's young surfers begin their careers. The Ditch can be surfed in any wind but only an hour either side of high tide.

There are good beach breaks between The Bar and Lion Rock and often a spitting right-hand bank forms that breaks best at mid to high incoming. The best time of the year to watch for it is from February through to May.

North Piha is the longer of the two beaches and beach breaks can be found at intervals along its length. There are several places that produce good banks: in the south there is often a left-hander from the back of Lion Rock; the helicopter pad is another spot; the rivermouth halfway up the beach another, and at the far northern end there is a break called **Caves**. All of these breaks work better than south Piha in smaller swells. Swells of 0.6 to 1.5 m from the north-west through to southerly will provide good waves, but the banks are fickle all year round. North Piha is best in lighter offshores from the north-east to south-east on an incoming tide.

KAREKARE BEACH

Appropriately, the name Karekare means 'rippling surf'. The beach is on the west coast about 4 km south of Piha and 35 km south-west of central Auckland. Its black sands stretch between two headlands, forming a central area of dunes. Streams empty into the sea at both ends of the beach, but the southern stream is often dry. Behind the beach there are some excellent bush walks and waterfalls.

Access to the beach is from the road to Piha down a steep and often narrow winding road. Drive carefully; there have been more accidents on this stretch of road than many surfers would care to remember. There is a carpark at the bottom of the road. From here the beach is about a 400-m walk down the stream bed past the surf club. To the south are the remains of the old Parahara railway, abandoned back in 1886. The railway was used to haul timber from Karekare through to Whatipu.

There are no camping facilities, shops or petrol here; the nearest facilities are back over the hill and north to Piha Beach. Karekare has an excellent surf lifesaving club which has its work cut out during the busy summer months. The beach is notoriously dangerous, with rips and holes continually forming up and down it.

Karekare can be divided into three main surf areas. At the northern end is a rocky outcrop that often has a good bank beside it. It forms fast right-handers and slower lefts and is best on a 1- to 1.5-m swell on a low to mid incoming tide. Karekare faces the west and picks up any westerly swell, but it is susceptible to strong winds. Offshores are straight easterlies or south-easterlies. The northern breaks are all right in north-easters but the southern part of the beach can get crossed up in strong winds from this direction.

The middle of the beach is made up of a series of beach breaks. It is very unpredictable and more often than not has no form. When there are good banks the beach can provide very fast and very hollow cylinders on the high tide. When the tide turns and starts going out, the beach becomes messy, full of holes and strong rips, especially if the swell is over 1.2 m. It is best on an incoming tide in waves from 1 to 1.5 m.

At the south end of the beach is probably the most consistent and best wave that the beach can offer. The best time of year is August through to January. It is a very heavy left-hand barrel that peels from beside the island for up to 100 m depending on the sand. It is best surfed on a low incoming tide in a 1.2- to

1.8-m swell. Best entry point is south of the break between the bank and the island. Light easterly winds are best and when this spot is cranking the tubes are some of the best you will find. They are fast and heavy and break over a very shallow sandbar. The rip travelling through the break adds to the power and makes staying in position very difficult. This is not a wave for beginners.

③ WAIKATO

The Waikato has a very interesting western coastline from the mouth of the Manukau Harbour south of Auckland to Kawhia. It is home to probably New Zealand's best-known and most consistent point break, Raglan. Through the centre of the area flows New Zealand's longest river, the Waikato, which wends its way from Lake Taupo, more than 350 km north-west, through a series of eight hydro power stations, to empty into the sea at the only other well-recognised surf spot, Port Waikato.

The main city in the region is Hamilton. The area is also home to a world famous tourist draw, the Waitomo Caves, which are about 77 km south of Hamilton on SH3.

The Waikato has a very long western coastline with few known breaks, mainly because of its general inaccessibility. Long stretches of the coast are only accessible through local farms. The area of beaches south of the Manukau Harbour and to the north of Port Waikato has some excellent waves on small swells and most are relatively easy to get to. South of Port Waikato through to Raglan there is very limited access to the beaches and coast, but for those with a yearning for adventure, there are some excellent reefs, points and bays along this coast. If you're planning to hunt waves and need to cross farmland to gain access, remember to get the farmer's permission or you're likely to get an arse full of number 8 shot.

South of Raglan there are a number of breaks, including **Ruapuke**, that are reasonably well known to the locals but not surfed all that often. They all have good waves but require the right conditions to get good surf. Offshores and a south-west swell from 1 to 1.8 m will give you some good waves on this west-facing and exposed coast.

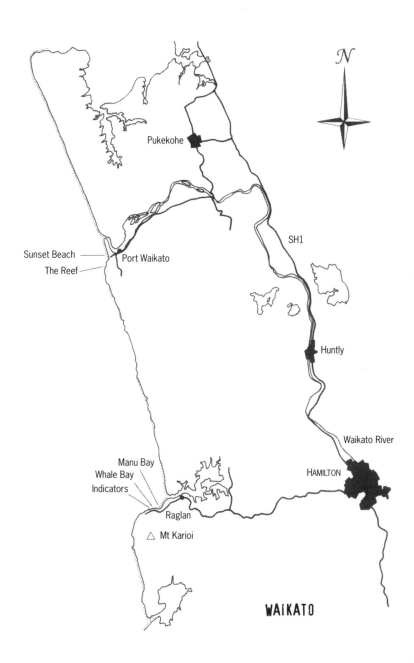

WAIKATO

PORT WAIKATO

Port Waikato lies on the sandy bar on the west coast at the mouth of the North Island's largest river, the Waikato. This little west coast holiday town was used as the base for the British forces when they were engaged in the wars against the Waikato Maori over a century ago. Port Waikato lies about one and a half hours south of Auckland and 32 km south-west of Tuakau. Petrol can be bought from one of several stores in the town, and takeaways, camping and accommodation are also available here. There is an excellent surf club at Sunset Beach and good fishing and mussels on the rocks south of the beach.

Sunset Beach is the west-facing beach that extends from the southern carpark north to the mouth of the Waikato River. It is best in a 0.6- to 1.8-m swell on an incoming tide with offshore winds coming in from the east or south-east. The beach is notorious for rips and holes, especially when the swell is on the larger side. All care should be taken, especially if the surf patrol is not active. The beach is best in the smaller swells which break on the many sandbars that constantly shift up and down the beach. Entry is easiest via one of the rips or holes between the different bars; getting out the back on the bigger swells can be quite difficult.

Further south around the rocks is **The Reef**, a heavy left-hander. It works best in a 1.8- to 2.5-m swell at low tide in light south-easterly or easterly winds. Access is by walking south from Sunset Beach about 1 km till you come to a steep rockface best negotiated at low tide. The Reef breaks from the other side of this rock outcrop north towards the beach. Entry is extremely difficult and can be made from in front of the take-off below the rock viewing area or from the little bay just north. Either way, you should only attempt surfing here if you are a strong duck-diver. If you get caught inside, there are only jagged rocks to come in on. It is best to watch some of the locals before attempting entry or exit.

The wave starts as a very heavy drop and barrel section; its difficulty is increased the deeper you dare to make the take-off. Following the first section, the wave peels off down the rocky point towards the beach for several hundred metres.

The Reef is only good in big, clean swells and is susceptible to strong offshore winds. It breaks over a shallow, broken reef and sand bottom and is good for most of the year. This break is notoriously heavy and is better left to experienced surfers.

RAGLAN

The township of Raglan lies about 48 km west of Hamilton on SH23. Raglan is a sleepy little fishing and farming town that has become one of New Zealand's premier surf locations. Nestled on the shores of Raglan Harbour, the town offers all the amenities needed if you intend to stay for any length of time. It has an excellent pub, good food provisions and a good camping ground.

Surfing started here way back in the early sixties and has continued to grow in popularity since. On the international surfing scene Raglan *is* New Zealand, and one of the major contributors to its fame is Raglan's consistency.

All the breaks of Raglan face to the north or north-west and peel down a series of left-hand points over a mixture of sand, reef and boulders. In New Zealand's predominant south-west winds Raglan offers surfers some of the only ridable waves while all around is onshore. Raglan is ridable in waves from 1 to 2.4 m although it can hold up to 3 m. Due to the angle of the breaks the swell is usually a lot smaller than waves elsewhere on the coast. A forecast of 2 to 3 m offers the best 1- to 1.8-m conditions since waves from the south-west lose a lot of size as they wrap around the headland under the shadow of Mt Karioi.

Driving into Raglan township, turn left at the bottom of the hill and keep heading along the main road west. Raglan's surf breaks are set among the private homes and farms of a little coastal community about 6 km south-west of the town.

The Point, or **Manu Bay**, is the first break as you head out along the road. It is a left-hander that wraps around a small headland, down a rocky point right in front of the carpark and into Manu Bay. It is best in waves from 1 to 1.8 m in offshore winds blown from the south-east. The Point is surfable in winds from light north-east through to south-west and even light westerlies. The waves are best on the lower tide, and the lower the tide the hollower the wave. As the tide comes in the wave becomes fuller but still offers excellent surfing. **The Ledge** is a shallow section out by the take-off area, and as the tide drops it can produce an exciting section. Take-off should be made either side of the ledge as trying to take off over it will almost always end in a pitching. Shoulder hoppers taking off from past the ledge should always beware of surfers either coming around the section or through it as most of the local hotties can easily negotiate it and often get barrelled here. Negotiation of the ledge is extremely difficult and should be left to the experienced.

Entry can be made by paddling out from the carpark across the line of breaking waves; by jumping out from the rock ledge beyond the break; or, for the less skilled, by paddling out from the boat ramp in Manu Bay. Ease of entry means this break can get very crowded, so if you are a below-average surfer stay well clear of the locals and experienced surfers. There are plenty of places to learn where the crowds aren't so heavy.

The next break is **Whale Bay**, affectionately known as Snail Bay. This is another good left-hand point that is best in waves 1.2 to 1.8 m in east to south-west winds. Whale Bay can hold 2.4 m plus, but once over 1.8 m it becomes slow, especially on the high tide. The break is best at half tide and entry can be made from either the rock shelf that extends down from below the grassed bank viewing area or out through The Valley to the west and paddling across into the line-up. Entry can be extremely difficult in bigger swells and a sound ability to duck-dive is a must for surfing here. The wave begins quite full from the take-off and picks up as it reaches a rock ledge in line with the rock shelf that extends from the grassed area. This ledge can produce some spectacular viewing as surfers try to negotiate it on an outgoing tide. Inside the ledge the waves rifle off and continue to offer good rides.

Beyond Whale Bay is **The Valley**, which is basically the inside section of **Indicators**. Indicators is the longest wave at Raglan and is almost always 0.3 to 0.6 m bigger than the others. It is best in waves from 1.2 to 2.4 m and a south or south-easterly wind. Indicators is more exposed than Whale Bay and The Point and is more susceptible to higher winds. It can provide the hollowest of Raglan's waves, peeling down a long boulder point for several hundred metres before reaching The Valley, where it continues to peel off before finally sectioning off across the rocks and beginning again at Whale Bay.

Entry is best made via The Valley and a long paddle to outside Indicators where the waves begin breaking. Entry can be difficult in bigger swells and, as with Whale Bay, a sound knowledge of duck-diving is essential.

GREAT BARRIER ISLAND

Great Barrier Island is situated about 20 km to the north of the Coromandel Peninsula and is the largest of the North Island's offshore islands. It covers some 285 square kilometres and is about 40 km long. Its eastern coastline features a rugged combination of cliffs, reef and white sandy beaches, very similar to the Coromandel except that the Barrier picks up significantly more swell than its neighbouring surf region. The surf on Great Barrier is often 0.3 to 0.6 m bigger than on the Coromandel and its beaches are more sheltered, with surfable conditions including south-easterly winds.

Great Barrier is one of the east coast's best surfing areas. Although not as predictable as the west coast, when the surf is up the banks are almost always good. Barrier has always been known for shark sightings as the crystal clear waters resemble Australia's Gold Coast, unlike our west coast where passing sharks often go unnoticed in the dirty water.

Great Barrier has many attractions other than the surf. It is home for a growing community and a holiday spot for many. It hosts an abundance of marine life and boasts excellent diving and fishing, so if you're planning a trip to Barrier a fishing line or diving gear is a must. The island also features hot springs, good pig hunting, bush walking and tramping, historic kauri dams and one of the deepest and largest natural harbours in the South Pacific, Port Fitzroy.

Facilities on the island include petrol, general stores in several settlements, accommodation at a backpackers', motels, home-stays and numerous camping areas. There are also plenty of rental baches available through Auckland newspapers. There are taxi and tourist bus services although they are an expensive means of transport. Hitchhiking, mountain biking and walking are probably the best ways to get around if you don't bring your own vehicle.

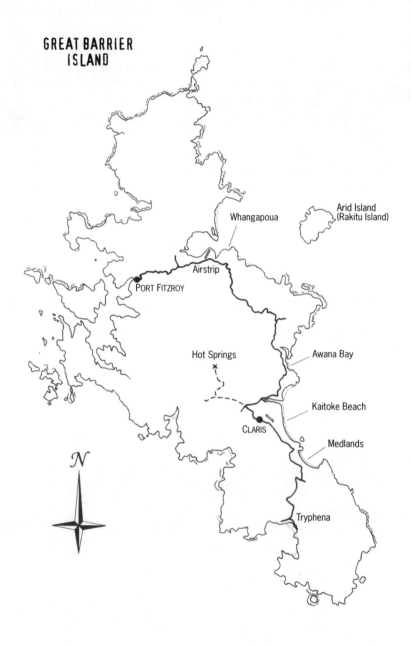

GREAT BARRIER
ISLAND

Whangapoua

Arid Island
(Rakitu Island)

Airstrip

PORT FITZROY

Hot Springs

Awana Bay

Kaitoke Beach

CLARIS

Medlands

N

Tryphena

However, the major surf breaks are a considerable distance apart and getting to them when conditions are right can be quite an exercise if you don't have your own transport.

The roads are almost all gravel, narrow and windy. The people of Great Barrier are quite different from the mainlanders, and are friendly provided you respect them, their property and the environment.

Great Barrier can be reached in various ways. There are several airstrips on the island, two within 15 minutes' walk of some of the best surf breaks. One is at Claris, close to the beaches of Medlands and Kaitoke Beach, and the airstrip at Okiwi is only a short walk from Whangapoua. There are several sea links to Auckland too. Fullers offer rapid transport to Tryphena and Fitzroy and a second company offers vehicle and passenger transport by car ferry.

If you intend travelling to Barrier for any length of time or with a group, the value of taking your own transport outweighs the very reasonable cost of the return ferry trip for a car. It is also a good idea to take as much of your provisions as you can, as costs on the island are greatly inflated. The camping areas on the island have few or no facilities, so all cooking must be done on barbecues provided or on your own portable gas stoves. Fires are strictly prohibited unless lit in marked areas or in the fireplaces provided.

WHANGAPOUA

Whangapoua is a right-hand bar on the mouth of the Whangapoua Estuary. It breaks over a very shallow sandbank across the mouth of the estuary from the rocky cliffs at the southern end of the bay across into the beach. It is also known as **Okiwi** and is very fast and hollow, breaking best on a low outgoing tide, but it can be surfed on any tide. It is best from 1.2 to 1.8 m in a north-easterly swell. The bar is good for most of the year. When the sand is in the right place the bar can provide some of the best barrels in the country, and even when the sand is not so good it is still a good wave.

The bar faces north and picks up any swell from the north-east through to the south-east. Offshore winds are southerly, south-westerly or light westerlies. Best access to the bar is from the airstrip out across the tidal flats of the estuary, but if the tide is high or incoming access can be difficult as the current runs swiftly. In this case, skirt the coast to the south to gain access.

To get through the surf, you can paddle out from the beach through the line-up, head out through the channel on an outgoing tide or jump off the rocks to the south. The wave starts as a very hollow and fast barrel and to make it the surfer must pull up into the tube straight off the mark. The wave then fires off across the bar to form long steep walls.

Hazards to watch for are the rip, the sharks and your board when you get nailed in the tube.

AWANA

Awana is the next well-known surf beach to the south and has a very steep profile. It has a reef in the southern corner of the bay and is mainly short, fast, hollow and very heavy beach breaks. It can be surfed in waves from 0.6 to 2.4 m and faces the east. The best swells come in from the north-east to the south-east and offshores blow from the west quarter. The beach is best surfed on the incoming tide, which provides punchier, bigger and more even surf.

Awana can be surfed all year round when there is swell and the sandbanks are always on the move, providing different waves every time you surf there. There is a camping ground at the northern end of the bay with a water supply that should be boiled before drinking.

KAITOKE BEACH

This is the main and largest beach on the east coast of Barrier. From **Palmers Beach** in the northern corner down to Pitokuku Island in the south, there are a multitude of good beach breaks. The bay can be surfed in any swell from the north to the south-east, in size ranging from 0.6 to 2.4 m. However, when the surf gets big surfers should check carefully the bar they intend surfing as the beach can get very rippy in a big swell. Depending on where you are surfing, offshores can blow from the north to the south-east.

Areas to watch for good bars are: the Kaitoke Creek mouth and the reefs around this area; the northern corner of Palmers Beach in a south-east swell; and the south end around Pitokuku Island in big north or north-east swells.

MEDLANDS

Medlands is the closest beach to the southern west coast port of Tryphena, and curves around to face north-east and north. During small north-east or northerly swells there are good banks all along the beach; these are best surfed on the incoming tide. In the southern corner of the bay is **Shark Alley**, a heavy right-hander that breaks over a reef and then walls up to peel across reef and sand to the beach break. It is best surfed in a northerly or north-easterly swell from 1.5 to 3 m. The break faces north and is offshore even in a south-east wind. There is easy access through the channel to the east of the reef and it is best surfed on an incoming tide on a big swell. As the name suggests, the hazards are sharks, and heavy waves.

5 COROMANDEL PENINSULA

The Coromandel is a very scenic part of the country. It offers travellers a range of outdoor pursuits from mountain biking and tramping to diving and fishing.

The Coromandel also has a colourful history, with some of the greatest gold strikes in the country made in its rugged mountain range. Kauri logging was also a major part of its history and there are still some good stands scattered within the ranges.

Surfing on the Coromandel has been popular since virtually the beginning of the sport in New Zealand. The most popular spot from days past is Whangamata, which still has one of the country's largest concentrations of surf shops and surfboard manufacturers, and the masses still favour it as *the* place during the summer.

But all the beaches along this east coast get swell. The breaks listed are the better, more reliable and consistent or the more accessible breaks on the east coast. There are plenty more that get good waves and have fun surf, including the northern tip of the Coromandel, Waikawau Bay and Port Jackson, and in a big north swell the western coast of the peninsula can also get some fun little waves.

The Coromandel has a climate all its own. The Coromandel Range is high enough to affect local weather patterns and during the prevailing south-westerly winds the eastern side of the peninsula gets a lot of clear air. Clouds get trapped on the range and drop their rain in the hills, leaving the east coast dry and with much higher sunshine hours than the west. The climate is favourable for other activities too. The Coromandel is one of the highest marijuana-producing regions in the country and its clear blue waters offer top diving and fishing.

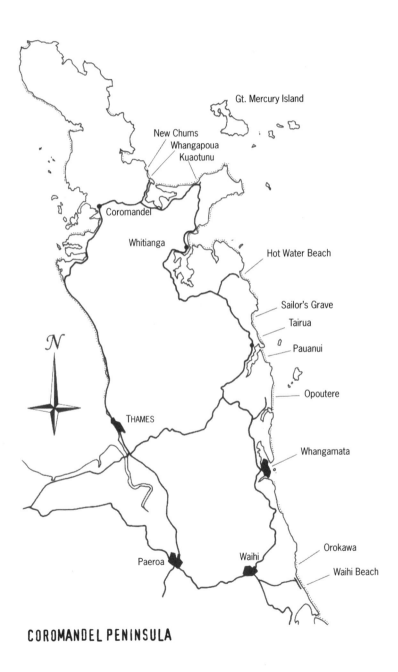

Gt. Mercury Island

New Chums
Whangapoua
Kuaotunu

Coromandel

Whitianga

Hot Water Beach

Sailor's Grave

Tairua

Pauanui

Opoutere

THAMES

Whangamata

Orokawa

Paeroa

Waihi

Waihi Beach

COROMANDEL PENINSULA

WHANGAPOUA

Whangapoua is a small settlement around the entrance of Whangapoua Harbour about 17 km north-east of Coromandel township. It boasts little in the way of amenities but the waves are good.

Whangapoua Beach faces north-east and is best surfed in swell from 0.6 to 1.5 m (though the swell forecast needs to be a lot bigger on the open coast for the swell to be 0.6 to 1.5 m here). Due to the sheltered location of the bay, the swell should be from the north or north-east, or a big easterly swell may manage to pass through the Mercury Islands that shelter the eastern approach to the bays in this location. There are a number of shifting banks up and down the beach that are best surfed on an incoming tide. Offshore winds are west or south-west and the best time to check these bays out is from February through to April when there are northerly swells coming off the Pacific cyclones.

Further north, either by way of a short walk or a paddle around the headland, is **New Chums**. This is a good beach break that breaks in the same conditions as Whangapoua but the beach profile is a little steeper and the waves are a little more powerful. During the late summer there is often a good right-hand bar at the south end of the bay, best surfed on the mid to high incoming tide.

Kuaotunu is a right-hand reef break on the road to the south of Whangapoua, about 24 km east of Coromandel and 17 km north-east of Whitianga. Just follow the road in to Kuaotunu on the way to Opito Bay and turn down to the boat ramp. The reef is straight out in front of the boat ramp and getting out is easy. It is an excellent wave when the swell is big enough to get into this sheltered spot. The reef faces due north and is offshore in a light south-west, southerly or south-easterly. The best time to check it out is during the huge north-easterly or northerly swells that come from tropical cyclones when the beaches to the south are too big. It is best from 1.2 to 2 m at any tide. However, it does get very shallow on the low tide. This wave, when it's on, is fast and very hollow — definitely worth a look.

HOT WATER BEACH

Hot Water Beach is about 30 km north of Tairua via SH25 to Whenuakite, turning off towards Hahei. There is an excellent camping ground by the beach and a shop that supplies the basic summer requirements. The nearest petrol and grocery store can be found at Hahei to the north. Back on SH25, also to the north, there is a pub at Coroglen. The other hotel close by is at Whitianga and a regular ferry can be caught from beyond Cooks Beach at Ferry Landing.

Hot Water Beach is so named because of the thermal activity present there. At low tide there is an outcrop of rocks several hundred metres north of the south end of the beach. Here hot water bubbles up through the sand. Tourists often come to soak in the hot mineral waters and build instant 'spas' by digging holes close to the springs at low tide. The camp ground also has several mineral spa pools available to the public for a nominal fee.

Hot Water Beach consists mainly of beach breaks on sandbars that come and go with the seasons. The south end also has a point break although it is dependent on sand build-up at the rivermouth to work well. When the sand is right the point works best on a half to full incoming tide in west or south-west winds. The point faces to the north-east and waves break over a mixture of boulders and sand. It breaks best in a 1- to 1.5-m swell from the east or north-east. Watch out for Vincents Rock out by the take-off spot as on a lower tide negotiation can get tricky. Best times of the year are from October through to March.

SAILORS GRAVE

Sailors Grave is a little hidden cove 5 km north of Tairua, the turn-off just at the top of the hill heading north. It was named after a sailor from the HMS *Tortoise* who drowned in the surf in the bay back in 1842, and his grave is in the rock outcrop just past the stream. Nestled among some of the Coromandel's most beautiful scenic coastal bush, the area is only slowly beginning to be developed. From the beach the Aldermen Islands can easily be seen to the south-east, and Shoe Island off to the south.

Sailors Grave consists mainly of sand beach breaks that change with the seasons. There are three main areas of surf — a right-hander at the south end of the bay that peels from a rocky reef into the bay, a right- and left-hand peak just to the north, and a left and right at the northern end of the bay. All these breaks are shifting all the time, but the best time of year to look out for good form on these banks is from October through to March. The banks are best on a mid to high incoming tide in any swell from north-east through to south-east. Because of the height of the hills surrounding Sailors, the bay can offer good conditions in the strongest of winds from south-west to north-west. Best swell size is from 1 to 2.4 m. Entry, especially in the bigger swells, can prove quite difficult and the best places to try from are the south end between the right-hander off the rocks and the next bank north, or further north again between the breaks. Watch the jagged rock shelves at the south end of the beach when paddling out and especially on your way in.

TAIRUA

Tairua is a rapidly growing holiday resort with a population that reaches saturation point during the summer. The town offers a selection of accommodation from upmarket motels through to camping grounds, and a range of other amenities to cater for the thousands of holidaymakers who flock to Tairua each summer. The harbour offers safe anchorage and separates Tairua from the nouveau riche resort of Pauanui. At the mouth of the Tairua River sits the 178-metre-high peak of Paku, which offers excellent views of both Pauanui and Tairua beaches. Tairua offers surfers plenty of alternatives when there is no surf. Several dive operations are based here and there is good fishing and seafood to be found on and around Tairua's beaches.

Tairua Beach is a steep white sand beach that can provide excellent beach breaks. It faces to the north-east and is best in a 1.2- to 1.8-m north-east or east swell on a mid incoming tide. Offshore is west or south-west although it is ridable in north-westerlies or light southerlies. The beach provides a series of beach breaks that can get very hollow, especially on larger swells. When the swell is up the beach is notorious for its strong undertows and rips and its steep profile adds power to the shore break, making getting out very difficult on those bigger days. The most consistent break on the beach is a right-hander in the lee of Paku, and the best time of the year to look out for it is from August to May. Tairua Beach waves are usually very fast with plenty of sections and heavy close-outs. Watch the rips.

Tairua Bar is a left-hand bar break that grinds off across the mouth of the Tairua River. Best access is from Pauanui either by driving around (25 km), catching the ferry from Tairua wharf, or by paddling across the rivermouth. This is a dangerous break as during the outgoing tide the river runs out at over 6 knots right through the break. It is also becoming more dangerous as the number of jet-skiers using the area increases. Watch these idiots, they have no idea. Other than that it is a fast left-hander that is best in a 1.2- to 2.4-m swell from the north-east or east. Surfing is best at dead low to low incoming tide with winds from the north-west to west, light south-west or northerly. When the bar is working well it can provide surfers with a fast barrelling wave, but beware of boats and remember to stay clear of the outgoing tide. It is recommended only for strong surfers.

Pauanui Beach is an east-facing beach, best in smaller swells from 0.6 to 1.5 m. The beach has much less incline than Tairua, making the waves easier. It is best from low incoming to full and provides a series of wandering bars as well as a right-hand point break at the far southern end. Offshore winds blow from west or south-west and the beach often shows its best form from October through to April.

OPOUTERE

Opoutere Beach is about 17 km north of Whangamata at the mouth of the shallow Wharekawa Harbour. The sandy dune and pine-forested foreshore is a bird and wildlife refuge so leave your dogs at home. The harbour has good floundering and plenty of shellfish. The beach is about 15 minutes' walk from the carpark through the sanctuary.

Opoutere has some good beach breaks, especially in a smaller swell. When other beaches are borderline for surfing there are often good little waves here. Best in a 0.6- to 1.2-m swell from any easterly direction in west to south-west winds and on an incoming tide. The shifting banks form hollow little rights and lefts up and down the beach. The best time to surf here is during the summer months when the consistent small swells build up the sand along the beach.

WHANGAMATA

Whangamata is probably one of the best-known (along with Raglan) surf spots in the country. It was a focal point during the early years of surfing in New Zealand, back in the sixties, and has never looked back. For all that has been written and said about the great Whangamata, it still doesn't get any more swell than any of the other beaches on the Coromandel. In fact, it is always 0.3 m or so smaller here than on the more northern Coromandel beaches. However, unlike the other beaches around here, Whangamata almost always has good banks when the swell is up.

Much of the hype about Whangamata comes from the enormous holiday population that swells the town to bursting point during the summer. It has become one of the premier holiday locations for Aucklanders and young party seekers and it is this that makes it a good place to stay away from during the summer holiday period. On a hot summer's day it is not unusual to see hundreds of young surfers and their families floundering in the waves.

The town has everything needed for an extended stay including a selection of surf shops and board manufacturers. The area has the usual holiday-type things to do should the sea be flat. Off the coast there is good diving at the islands in the bay and further afield via charter boat.

The surfing areas at Whangamata can be broken into three main spots. They all get swell from the north-east or east and the best time of the year is from January through to April when lows move over the top of New Zealand and the tropical cyclones head down our way from north Australia and the islands of the Pacific.

Whangamata Bar is probably the best-known wave here and is at the northern end of the beach across the mouth of the Whangamata Harbour. It is a left-hand bar that breaks best from 1.2 to 2.4 m in a north-easterly swell. It is best surfed on a low to mid incoming tide in offshores from the north-west to south-west. When conditions are right the bar can produce fast barrelling left-handers that peel for a hundred metres. Best access to the break is either out through the rip from the harbour to the right of the break on an outgoing tide (for more experienced surfers only) or by a straight paddle from the beach out along the line of the breaking waves. The waves break only over sand and the only real hazards in the water are the rip that runs through the take-off zone on an outgoing tide, or the beginners who insist on floating about and getting in the way. Surfing here can often be more of a skilled game of dodgems than the real thing. The best time to surf here is the off-peak season and midweek. The best viewing is from the dunes in front of the break or the carpark.

Whangamata Beach fills a scallop-shaped indentation that faces north-east. To the north is the bar and to the east are several islands that block out east-south-east swells. The beach can get very crowded during the summer with surfers, swimmers, malibus, wave-skis and clubbies. Don't surf between the flags, and if you do feel it is necessary to surf here during the summer holidays and you're smart, you'll wear a helmet.

There are always good banks on the beach that can be surfed on any tide, although invariably the waves are better on the incoming tide. The beach is best in a north-easterly swell from 0.6 to 1.5 m and offshore winds blow from the south-west quarter. The waves peak up on the sandbars and peel, usually quite full, through to the beach break where they pick up to barrel and dump onto the beach.

The Estuary is Whangamata's southernmost surf break. The Estuary empties into the sea on the south side of the town and can provide excellent right-hand waves. The break faces east and is offshore in a westerly or south-westerly. It is best surfed in a north-east or east swell from 1.2 to 1.8 m. The waves peel across a bar formed at the mouth of the estuary. The form of the waves depends a lot on the shape of the bar and the bar can often be no good at all. But when it has good form the waves are fast, hollow and offer excellent rides.

WAIHI

The township of Waihi is about 20 km east of Paeroa and 31 km south of Whangamata. An old gold town, it is the home of the Martha Mine, New Zealand's biggest gold strike.

Waihi Beach lies about 11 km east of the main town and is a community and holiday resort independent of Waihi town. The beach has garages, shops, takeaways and camping grounds and the northern end of the beach has a good surf lifesaving club. Waihi Beach is about 10 km long and faces the north-east. It has a fairly flat beach profile, making it best for surfing on smaller swells and on the mid to high incoming tide. It is best surfed in a north-east swell and waves from 0.6 to 1.5 m. The extreme ends of the beach offer the best spots to look for banks, though on small swells there are good banks all the way along the beach.

A 45-minute walk to the north lies **Orokawa Bay**. Access to the beach is only via the walking track that begins in the northern corner of Waihi Beach and wanders north over a series of steep ridges to descend to the bay. Orokawa Bay has a much steeper profile than Waihi and can offer better waves if the banks are good. It, too, is offshore in a west or south-west wind and picks up a north-easterly or easterly swell. The beach has varying banks that wander up and down it from swell to swell. The most consistent is a right-hander in the southern corner of the bay. Orokawa is best from 1 to 1.8 m on an incoming tide. The waves are fast and often hollow, ending in a sand-dredging beach break. When the surf is bigger there is a strong rip and undertow that swimmers and inexperienced surfers should be wary of. Remember that there is no surf patrol to bail you out should you get into trouble.

⑥ BAY OF PLENTY ▾

The Bay of Plenty is a large, mainly sandy coastal area that faces mostly north. There are a few rocky headlands that break up the long white sand beaches and it is around these headlands and harbour or rivermouths that many of the Bay's best waves are found. To the north-west the Bay begins with Matakana Island, whose waves have been well documented in surfing journals around the world. The bay then stretches east to the beginning of the East Cape area at the mouth of the Motu River.

The Bay of Plenty is, as the name suggests, a bountiful and agriculturally rich area. Its boundaries incorporate places like Te Puke, the home of the kiwifruit industry, Mt Maunganui, a growing seaside holiday resort, and White Island, an active volcanic island that continuously smoulders away in the bay. The area is also one of the richest game fishing areas in the country and surfers on the bar at Whakatane often catch glimpses of some of the great monsters of the depths as they pass by chained to the sterns of the game boats.

Although an exposed coastal region, the Bay is probably one of the less unreliable regions in terms of surf. Its northerly outlook requires strong easterly or north to north-easterly swells to get in. The waves surfed here are usually smaller and less powerful than in other areas. For instance, if there is a 2-m north-easterly swell running then the Bay will have good waves from 1 to 1.5 m, but on the Coromandel the waves will be 1.2 to 1.8 m and more powerful.

The entire Bay of Plenty gets waves when the swell is up, and the beaches are long and usually have plenty of banks. The surf breaks that are mentioned in this chapter are a few of the breaks that can produce good waves when the conditions are right. They are the better, more reliable or more accessible surf spots. The travelling surfer can venture down most of the roads to the beach and find waves when the swell is running.

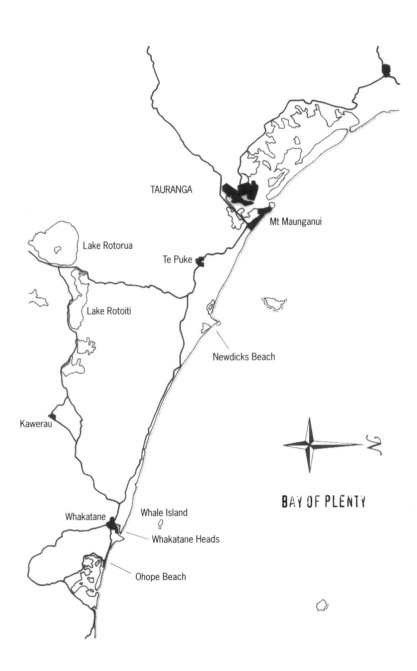

TAURANGA

Mt Maunganui

Lake Rotorua

Te Puke

Lake Rotoiti

Newdicks Beach

Kawerau

Whale Island

Whakatane

Whakatane Heads

Ohope Beach

BAY OF PLENTY

MATAKANA ISLAND

Matakana Island has gained a reputation overseas as one of the premier New Zealand surf locations, but this false image was born from the limited information available on New Zealand in overseas surfing publications. The photos of Matakana or Puni's Farm that put New Zealand on the world surfing map gained acceptance in these publications over other, often better waves because of the pristine blue water and tropical look that the island's surf has. It seems that when Matakana is good it is very good but most of the time, like the rest of the Bay, it is flat.

For the most part, the island consists of a large maturing pine forest with a small Maori community at the western end. Most of the island is Maori-owned and travelling surfers should respect their land. No camping is allowed unless permission is gained. The best means of access to the shores of Matakana is by boat. The island is a long paddle, one that is not recommended as the currents in the harbour and at the harbour mouths are treacherous. Boats can be chartered to take groups of surfers across from either Tauranga or Mt Maunganui.

Matakana's exposed northern coastline consists of a steep-profile golden sand beach that stretches from the Katikati entrance of the Tauranga Harbour in the west to the Tauranga entrance in the east. The waves are good at both ends of the beach and there are good banks along its entire length. When the surf is 0.6 to 1 m at the Mount the waves at Matakana are 0.3 m bigger, and because of the beach profile they are heavier and considerably hollower. Matakana is renowned for its barrels. The best time of the year to surf Matakana is during the late summer when the Bay gets most of its northerly and easterly swells. The island is best in waves from 1 to 1.8 m and on an incoming tide. The best time of the tide depends a lot on the size of the swell; if it is small it is best on low incoming, but the bigger the swell the higher the tide needs to be for the best form. The best swell direction is north-east and the best winds are light south-westerlies. The waves are short, very fast and very hollow. They peel off along the sandbars that create right- and left-hand peaks that jack up quickly to barrel off or create a steep, fast-breaking but makeable wall to the shore break.

MT MAUNGANUI

Mt Maunganui is one of New Zealand's major seaside holiday resorts. The Mount caters for thousands of tourists and holidaymakers who travel here each year to enjoy the sunshine, golden beaches and recreational facilities that include the Bay Park Raceway. The Mount lies on the sandy isthmus that joins the 230-metre-high volcanic promontory at Tauranga Harbour's entrance to the mainland to the east. It is accessible from Tauranga by the harbour bridge or by SH2, which travels around the harbour to the east.

The Mount's beaches are divided by Leisure Island, a small rocky outcrop joined to the mainland by the sand. The island serves as an easy entry point should the waves in the bay get big. To the west of Leisure Island lies the main Mt Maunganui Beach while to the east Ocean Beach stretches off to the horizon.

The main beach is the centre of activity for practically the whole of the Mount's population. It has a major surf lifesaving club plus all the icecream, food and entertainment establishments anyone could want. There is a good camping ground at the base of the Mount fronting the western end of the beach. Opposite is the Oceanside Hotel, while on the same side of the road are the hot pools. When the surf is up here during the summer months the crowds are beyond belief. Everyone takes to the water to ride the waves in every conceivable type of contraption. **Main Beach** is best in a northerly or north-easterly swell from 1 to 1.8 m on an incoming tide. There are two places that often have good waves and they lie at either end of the beach. The beach has quite a steep profile at high tide and in the smaller swells this can provide some entertaining surfing, with surfers riding a wave to the beach and then stepping off their boards from the shore break onto the sand.

South of Leisure Island is the long expanse of **Ocean Beach** as it heads east down to the headland at Maketu. The beach is a gently sloping white sand beach that offers surfers a variety of banks that change with each new swell. The beach is surfable in any north or north-easterly swell from 0.6 to 1.8 m in winds from the south-west through to south. Ocean Beach can be surfed on any tide although there are often better waves on the incoming tide, especially if the swell is bigger than 1.2 m. The beach is easily accessible along Marine Parade or through the many accessways from Ocean Beach Rd. It is also accessible to the east at various places off Papamoa Beach Rd and at Papamoa itself. Places that are worth checking when the swell is running are

Tay St, opposite the dairy; the surf club at Omanu; and east down the coast at **Papamoa**.

NEWDICKS BEACH

Newdicks is a privately owned beach on the eastern side of Town Pt and Maketu township. There are good waves at the Maketu Bar providing the sand is good, but Newdicks can often produce better beach breaks. Newdicks is about 2 km from Maketu and is open to the public from 7 am to 5 pm every day during the summer. There is a gate charge for the use of the road and during the winter there is an honesty box. Use it and surfers will continue to be allowed to come and surf here. If the road is closed the beach is still accessible via a walking track. Getting there by road is relatively easy. Take the Maketu Beach road from SH2 through to Maketu and on past the monument commemorating the landing of the *Arawa* canoe for a further 1.5 km to Newdicks access, which is signposted.

Maketu is one of the oldest Maori settlements in the Bay of Plenty. It is thought that the *Arawa* canoe made landfall at the mouth of the Kaituna River back in the mid-14th century. The area has always been the stronghold of the Arawa people and the area's marae have some of the finest carved meeting houses in the country.

Newdicks beach is best in a north-easterly or easterly swell with winds from the south-west or west. The best size is from 1 to 1.8 m on a low incoming tide although the surf is often good on all tides. The beach features a series of rocky outcrops which can often create good sandbanks. The surf breaks mostly over sand, with a little reef here and there. There is no particular area of the beach that gets better waves, as the banks change and move around with each new swell. Newdicks is often surfed when westerly conditions prevail as, along with Ohope, it offers the only sheltered surf in the area if winds are strong.

WHAKATANE

Whakatane is a large town situated in the central bight of the Bay of Plenty. All amenities can be found only a couple of kilometres from the surf. The town is situated at the base of a rocky headland that extends several hundred metres into the sea. The Whakatane River flows out on the western side of the headland and is a popular port for fishing and game fishing boats. The port's boats offer game fishing, diving and hapuku fishing in and around Whale Island (out to the north of the bar) and the active volcano White Island, which can be seen smoking on the horizon.

Whakatane Bar is one of the best and most consistent right-hand breaks in the Bay of Plenty. It breaks all year round, with the sandbank producing waves between good and excellent most of the year during any northerly or north-easterly swell from 1 to 2.4 m. The bar is offshore in south to south-easterly winds and its waves break over a shallow sandbank that extends from the northern side of the river to a series of reefs that mark the edge of the harbour channel. The bar is best at low tide but if there is a good swell running the bar can be surfed on any tide. The wave begins with a fast section, followed by a steep and workable wall on which the ever-vigilant surfer can always find a barrel or two. When the sand is good, the bar can fire for over a hundred metres. Getting out can be fun as surfers must first cross the river in which the biggest hazard are the boaties, so watch out for them. During the winter the river can be several degrees below the temperature of the sea and keeping the hands and feet free from numbness is quite an art. Watch the rip and start paddling far enough up or down the bank so that you reach the opposite bank and don't end up out to sea or halfway up the river.

OHOPE

Ohope Beach is on the eastern side of Whakatane Heads and stretches east about 15 km to the entrance of Ohiwa Harbour. Ohope township is mainly a holiday resort and is the next stop east of Whakatane on the coast. There are camping grounds, motels, shops and petrol, and just a short drive south of the beach on the banks of the Ohiwa Harbour is an oyster farm that has great oysters as well as plenty of fresh seafood. They do a mean fish, oysters and chips meal.

Ohope Beach is a very flat-profiled beach and is therefore not good in big swells. The beach is best surfed in swell from the north to north-east around the 0.6- to 1.2-m mark. It will also handle a slightly bigger swell at the western end on a mid to high tide. There are banks up and down the beach but often the best form can be found on the banks at the western end. The banks form good fast-breaking right- and left-hand peaks that can produce some good fast little waves. Offshores blow from the south-west to south-east while the western corner is also protected in a westerly.

TARANAKI

Taranaki is one of the country's top surfing areas. Its consistency and varied surf breaks make it the number one location for the serious surfer looking for waves. The coast curves around snow-capped Mt Egmont to supply surfers with surf breaks that face from north through to south, making it possible to surf this area in almost all winds except a straight westerly. The coast to the north of New Plymouth consists mainly of long beaches broken by headlands and river and estuary entrances. Up the coast the beach has a slightly flatter profile, making it not quite as good as south of New Plymouth in bigger swells. To the south begins the huge lava shelf from the volcano Mt Egmont (also known as Mt Taranaki). This shelf creates countless surf breaks that peel off into small beaches and boulder bays over rocky shelves and reefs. There are hundreds of spots that have good waves and remain relatively unsurfed. The breaks listed in this guide are only a few of the better known, more accessible and reliable locations on the coast. For the travelling surfer the rugged coast between the access roads can offer good reef waves that break in most westerly swells and can handle a wide range of wave sizes. Every Taranaki surfer has his or her own special secret break on this coast and there are plenty to choose from.

The main centre in Taranaki is New Plymouth. The city has a population of over 40,000 and has all the amenities a surfer could possibly need. There are surf shops and camping grounds on the main town beach, Fitzroy, and a range of other activities to entertain surfers between the swells. To the north is the gas-to-petrol plant, Motunui, the McKee oil field, a gas-to-methanol plant and, offshore, the Maui natural gas field. Coming towards New Plymouth from the north the surf breaks begin where the road first reaches the coast at the Awakino River mouth. There are surf spots on the beaches, headlands and rivermouths all along the coast from here to New Plymouth. South of New Plymouth SH45 takes you around the coastal plains below Mt Egmont to Hawera where the road joins SH3 to continue down the coast to Wanganui.

Weather around the Taranaki coastline can often be bleak, but for hardcore surfers there are always good waves to be had no matter what the weather brings. If it is flat then there is always another swell only a day or two away. The time of year only affects the weather, which is best in late summer and autumn. In the summer the water is warm and spring suits are ample unless a south-easterly or southerly is blowing the cold down off the mountain. It pays to be prepared and equipped for all conditions. The winter requires a good steamer, and booties are always a bonus over the reefs and for getting in and out over the rocky entry points at many of the breaks.

Many of the breaks require crossing farmland to gain entry. Check with the farmer first; they will always appreciate your courtesy. And remember to close the gates behind you.

FITZROY BEACH

Fitzroy is the main beach for New Plymouth city and faces the north-west. The suburb of Fitzroy has two camping grounds with cabin accommodation — one at Belt Rd overlooking Port Taranaki and the other, Fitzroy Camp, on Beach St. Both camps are good, close to the city, yet on the beachfront.

Fitzroy is a steeply profiled sand beach that stretches from the port breakwater in the west along the boundary of the city east-north-east towards Bell Block. The beach is best surfed in a north-westerly or westerly swell, but a big south-westerly swell can also wrap around the Port Hills to hit the beach's banks. The beach is best surfed in waves from 1 to 2.4 m and on the high tide in bigger swells. The offshores blow from the south or south-east off the mountain and during the winter surfing here can be a chilling experience. The waves are usually very heavy and hollow with the negotiation of the beach break creating quite a few problems for inexperienced and experienced alike when the swell is over 1.5 m. Right- and left-hand peaks peel and close out off the many banks that form up and down the beach, with some of the best banks being found around Beach Rd and the Fitzroy Camping Ground. When the swell

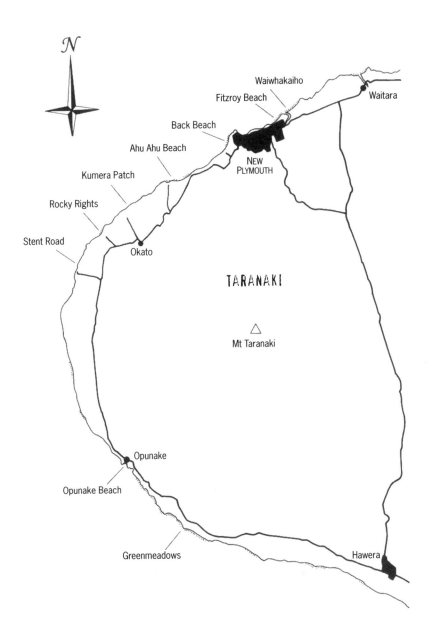

Waiwhakaiho

Fitzroy Beach

Waitara

Back Beach

Ahu Ahu Beach

NEW
PLYMOUTH

Kumera Patch

Rocky Rights

Stent Road

Okato

TARANAKI

△
Mt Taranaki

Opunake

Opunake Beach

Greenmeadows

Hawera

is big there are also good waves at the more protected Belt Rd end of the beach. The further north-east you travel, the less protected the beach becomes and the bigger the swell. Fitzroy is an excellent wave when conditions are right and can provide surfers with some good barrels.

WAIWHAKAIHO

At the northern end of Fitzroy Beach is Waiwhakaiho, a good bombora-type reef break on the northern side of the Waiwhakaiho River mouth. It is good in all swells and best on an incoming tide from middle to high. The waves break over a shallow reef right and left and can peel for up to 100 m, the left being the better and longer ride. The reef can handle waves from 1.2 through to 2.4 and 3 m.

BACK BEACH

Back Beach is the second town beach of New Plymouth. It sits in the hook to the south of Port Hills and is the home of the Taranaki Boardriders' headquarters. It is easily reached from the city by heading out of the suburbs on SH45 a couple of kilometres and turning right at the road signposted Beach and Gun Club.

Back Beach faces west-south-west and has a steep profile that creates good punchy waves on most tides. The beach consists of sand that shifts about continuously to produce consistently good banks. It is best in waves around the 0.6- to 1.8-m mark, but if the banks are good it can handle up to 2.4 m. Best tides are generally incoming to high. However, on the flatter days, i.e., 0.6 to 1.2 m, there are often banks that are good on all tides. The best offshores blow from the north to south-east and the bay is sheltered quite well from winds from the top or the bottom of the compass.

AHU AHU BEACH

Ahu Ahu Beach is the first of the main breaks south of Oakura. It is easily accessible from Ahu Ahu Rd, about 2.5 to 3 km south of Oakura, which takes you down to the beach. The beach itself has a reasonable beach break that can be quite heavy even in small waves. The bay is relatively deep so the waves hit both the reefs and the beach quite hard. The bay has two reef breaks as well. There is a right-hander at the northern end of the bay and a good left at the southern end of the beach. It is best on a low incoming tide in winds from the south or south-east. Ahu Ahu can be surfed in any swell from north-west to big south but isn't too good in swell much over 1.5 m, though the reefs to the south are.

KUMERA PATCH

Kumera Patch is rated as one of the best left-handers in Taranaki. It is a magical left-hand point break that can peel for 100 to 150 m along a rugged boulder bank. It is a top to bottom wave that has a solid pocket and long wall. Kumera Patch is best in swell from the south-west and winds from the south to south-east. It holds from 1 to 3 m and is best at low tide in waves from 1.8 to 2.4 m. Getting there is a little more difficult. There is a road at the bottom of the dip before you turn the corner into Okato, heading south. The road stops about 1 km short and the rest of the trip is on foot. Ask the farmer's permission before heading over his land.

ROCKY RIGHTS

Next is Rocky Rights and Rocky Lefts. They are at the end of Paora Rd, a few kilometres south of Okato. The road takes you to a small carpark at its end and from there the bay is a walk of around 500 m. Go over the fence and head across the paddock south to the bay. Rocky Rights breaks right in front of the bank and peels off a reef into the deep boulder bay. **Rocky Lefts** is the other side of the bay and does the same but in reverse. Entry is easy as the inside of the bay is quite deep and the boulder bank steep. However, getting back in a big swell can be a little testing on the nerves as the heavy surge up and down the boulders makes getting your footing a little difficult. Rocky Rights will work on most tides and the bigger the swell the fuller the tide needs to be. It works best on a north-westerly or westerly swell in waves from 1 to 2.4 m in winds from the north-east to east, while Rocky Lefts breaks best from 1 to 1.8 m in swell from south-west to west and winds from south-east to east. Both waves have a good bowling pocket and workable wall. They can often provide a tube or two and always have plenty of power.

Remember to consult the farmer before venturing across his land. At a lot of these breaks it is not necessary, but if you are surfing here for the first time, or the first time in a while, it doesn't hurt to be polite. Finding these breaks can be difficult, so it is best to stop in at one of the local surf shops in either New Plymouth or Oakura and ask.

STENT RD

Stent Rd is south of Okato on SH45 and is well signposted. The road takes you to the coast north of Cape Egmont. When you reach the beach veer to the right. A driveable track travels north about 800 m to a carpark right in front of the surf break. The nearest accommodation is at the pub at Okato or the camping ground at Oakura.

Stent Rd is a very good and consistent right-hand reef break. It breaks over shallow boulders and reef on a rocky point and peels through into a steep boulder bay. It faces west-south-west and picks up every south, west or north-west swell that hits the coast. It is offshore in north-easterlies through to south-easterlies and is best in waves from 1 to 2.4 m. Stent is a very heavy wave in bigger swells and is best surfed on an incoming tide.

Entry can be made via the inside bay; the surfer can then paddle out through the shore break to the line-up out the back. Best viewing is from the banks around the carparks. On the low tide the reef is very shallow and on the low incoming tide it can produce excellent barrels. Stent may be surfed at any time of the year when the winds are offshore.

OPUNAKE BEACH

Opunake Beach is often a good spot to check out for heavy beach breaks. The bay is the town beach for Opunake and has a surf lifesaving club. There are garages and a good pub in the town and a camping ground at the beach, but no cabins. The beach is offshore in winds from the north to north-east and best in a 1- to 2.4-m swell from the south-west. It is best surfed on an incoming tide but is surfable on all tides. The beach has a series of peaks whose form varies from swell to swell. When the bay is on there are often some good fast-breaking barrels to be had and long walls. The beach also has its own big wave break that can handle waves up to 3.7 m, and sometimes (if the conditions are right) a little bigger. **Desperation Point** is mainly a right-hand reef break at the end of the bay but it also has a reasonable left. This break is fairly unpredictable and is a reasonably short ride but if you get it when it's on, the drops are worth the paddle.

GREENMEADOWS

Greenmeadows is one of the better-known breaks to the south of Opunake, but is by no means the only good wave. There are good waves on the reefs at **Sky Williams**, **Mangahume** and the many other reefs and bays in between. Greenmeadows is a long right-hand point that favours a south or south-west swell. It can hold a swell up to 3 m while the bay inside is good in waves from 1 to 1.5 m. The point is offshore in winds from the north or north-east and is a fullish wave that can have some good sections. It peels along a long boulder and rock reef and can be surfed on most tides. For the best form the swell needs to be up around the 1.8- to 2.4-m mark. Access is again over farmland and permission is needed. Heading south from Opunake, follow the main road past Waitino Rd on the left; shortly after, the road veers to the left and down to a bridge over a stream. On the left after the stream is a rest area in some trees and you can park anywhere around here. Follow the river to the coast and you're there. The farmer's house is a little further south on the right and, when asked politely, he will often allow surfers to drive to the point across his land.

South of Greenmeadows there are numerous breaks and most roads that lead to the coast along this stretch to Wanganui have waves at their ends. As the coast curves further south towards Paraparaumu the surf gradually takes a turn for the worse, becoming progressively smaller and less consistent. South-west and south swells are blocked by the South Island and any swell that does get in is lost on the shallow shelf that extends offshore. There are still good waves on this stretch of coast when conditions are right, but they are less predictable and harder to find.

⑧ GISBORNE

isborne is one of the most out-of-the-way places in the North Island. Getting there from any direction by road involves a long and winding journey. Avoid SH38 which, though it looks shorter, takes twice as long and is three times as windy, with the small consolation of being more scenic. But the trip to Gisborne is worth it as it is as close as New Zealand comes to a surf town.

Gisborne sits at the northern end of Poverty Bay, which gives the town a south- and an east-facing coastline. Both coasts are only a bike ride from the centre of town. The town has a number of surfboard factories and numerous surf shops. There are swell reports every morning on the local radio station and almost always a wave to be had. The coast picks up all the easterly and north-easterly swell while at the same time picking up the southerly and south-easterly swells that roll up the coast from the lows that constantly pass under the South Island.

To the north lies East Cape, and for surfers who have a few spare days a mission around the Cape can be rewarded with good waves. Although not listed in this guide, there are certainly plenty to be had. From the **Motu River** mouth on the north-western side around to Hicks Bay and south down the coast there are hundreds of good breaks. Hollow fast-breaking beach breaks alternate with some very good reef breaks on the headlands and rocky shore that separates the many golden sand beaches. East Cape has the added attraction of being relatively deserted for most of the year. For tourists it is a must. Places like **Waipiro Bay**, **Tokomaru Bay**, **Tolaga Bay** and all the bays and reefs in between have good waves and are worth a look.

Gisborne has some of the best weather on offer to surfers, especially during the prevailing westerlies that flow over New Zealand. During the summer months the beaches are very hot and the water warm. Spring suits or vests are

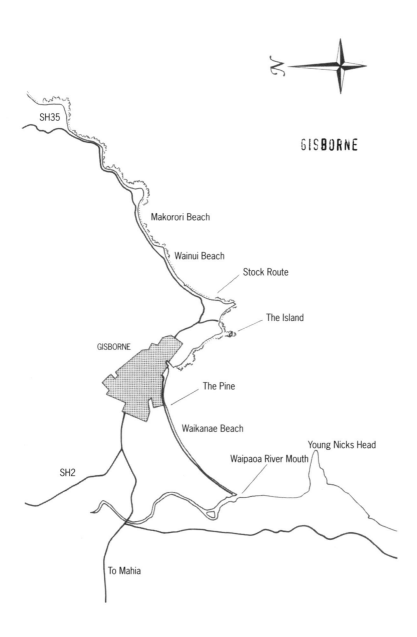

GISBORNE

SH35

Makorori Beach

Wainui Beach

Stock Route

The Island

GISBORNE

The Pine

Waikanae Beach

Young Nicks Head

Waipaoa River Mouth

SH2

To Mahia

usually enough to keep out the chill during the hot and sunny season, but when a southerly change takes place the weather rapidly deteriorates and temperatures drop quickly. During the winter the water is cold and often the winds are even colder, so steamers and often booties are required for comfortable surfing.

MAKORORI

Makorori Beach is a few kilometres north of Wainui Beach on SH35. At the end of Wainui the road winds up over a small headland and into the sweep of Makorori. Makorori Beach is notorious for the jagged reef that surfers must negotiate to get out, especially at low tide. The northern end has a small settlement of holiday-type houses and just to the north over the hill is Tatapouri and the Tatapouri Hotel. The hotel is right on the coast and a great place to stop in for a cold beer on a hot day. You can take your beer and sit on the grass overlooking the beach and the surf breaking on the maze of reefs that lie offshore.

At Makorori the beach can be divided into a series of breaks. Starting at the south end is **Makorori Point**, a long right-hand point break. It breaks over a shallow reef and is a slow and often full wave that can provide a long ride. Watch how far you get away from the pocket because as the wave curves around the reef surfers need to constantly cut back to stay with it. The wave is good for bodyboarding and long boards (malibus). The best part of the wave is usually the take-off and first section that walls up before peeling off to the beach. It is best in a south or south-east swell at low tide and can be ridden on higher tides on a bigger swell. The ideal size is from 1.2 to 2.4 m, with the best waves around the 1.8-m mark. The point is offshore in northerlies through to westerlies, but as it is a long way offshore it is susceptible to wind chop if the wind gets too strong. Best access is from the southern end of the bay under the trees out along the line of the breaking waves; it's a long paddle.

The next break is **Centres** which is the peak or peaks just north of the point. It is best on a high tide but is surfable on any tide. The waves break over a combination of reef and sand and the best size is from 1 to 1.8 m. The waves peak up over the reef and the sand bottom to form good rights and lefts that wall up and can sometimes provide a little tube.

The form of these breaks depends a lot on the sand that builds up on the rugged reef bottom but there are almost always good waves here all year round. The beach picks up most swells from north-east through to south and is best from 1 to 1.8 m; some of the peaks will handle a little bigger on a high tide. There are a further three named breaks north of Centres down the beach. Next is **Red Bus**, followed by **The Creek**. They are both good peaks and are subject to similar winds, swell and swell size as Centres.

North Makorori is sheltered in the northern curve of the bay. It is similar in conditions to the others except that it is more sheltered from a north-easterly through to north-westerly. West or south-west winds tend to get a little cross-shore here. Again there are reef and sand combination peaks that break in most swells. North Makorori is often good in an easterly or big north-easterly swell.

WAINUI BEACH

Wainui is the east-facing town beach for Gisborne and is about 6 km south-east of the town centre on Wainui Rd. Wainui has its own little community which is an extra suburb for Gisborne. It has petrol stations, food, takeaways, motels and a restaurant and bar, but no camping facilities. For the nearest camping, surfers need to head back into Gisborne to either the Waikanae Beach Motor Camp or Churchill Park.

Wainui Beach stretches from Tuaheni Pt in the south through to Makorori Pt in the north. At either end of the beach are large areas of low and rugged reef that slowly thin out towards the middle of the beach, but the moving sands often expose reef at intervals along the entire beach. So the surf breaks over a combination of sand and reef on a reasonably steep-profile beach.

Wainui Beach is best surfed in a north-easterly to south-easterly swell from 1 to 1.8 m. A big southerly swell can also wrap around to get in here. The beach is best on a mid to high incoming tide, but it offers reasonable waves on all tides. Offshore winds blow from north-west to south-west. The waves are fast and can get pretty heavy on the bigger swells from the south, especially on the outer banks. On a big swell places like the Stock Route and Pines can provide some awesome barrel sessions. The beach gets waves most of the year. This area of New Zealand rates alongside New Plymouth at the top of the consistency chart in terms of the high number of surfable days per year.

The beach can be divided into three main areas of surf. The first one at the south end is the **Stock Route**. It is easily accessible from the main road just as the road turns parallel to the beach to head north. Access is about 20 m past the service station. The Stock Route is probably the most popular and consistent surf spot on the beach. The waves here are best from 1 to 1.5 m in an easterly or south-easterly swell. A combination of reef and sand forms a hot right- and left-hand peak. Stock Route is also the most popular spot for the local competitions.

Further north there are a couple of accessways to the beach where there are good banks before you arrive at the Wainui Surf Lifesaving Club. On the northern side is a parking area and playground that sits on the top of the dunes in the pine trees. This area is called **Pines** and is another spot worth checking out for waves. On the beach below there is a series of reefs that run out from the beach, and the sand that builds up around them can create some good banks. Best here on any swell from 1 to 1.8 m on a mid incoming tide, and stay out of the clubbies' patrolled area or you'll end up with a wave ski implanted in your head.

At the northern end of the bay the sand gives way to mainly reef and there are some good waves to be had here on the low to middle tide in swell from 1.2 to 1.8 m. Often these reefs can hold even bigger if the winds aren't too strong and the sand is good. As the tide comes in the outer banks and reefs get too full and break into a deep hole off the beach. When the tide comes in either head back down to the Stock Route or north to Makorori Beach.

THE ISLAND

The Island is Gisborne's premier break. It is a left-hander that barrels off the back of Tuamotu Island at the western end of Sponge Bay. Access to The Island is via the road to Sponge Bay between Gisborne and Wainui Beach. Take the road to the end and park the car overlooking Sponge Bay. Make sure you lock all your valuables in the boot as the surf break is a long way from, and out of sight of, the car and the area is reasonably isolated. Over the bank to the west there is a track that leads down to a boulder bay on the western side of The Island. It is a very long paddle from here out and around the island to the break and the waves can't be seen from the carpark. If you're coming from Gisborne and want to check out The Island, then a quick trip up Kaiti Hill will give a somewhat distant but good overview of The Island and the waves beyond to the south-east.

The long paddle is worth it if you get The Island when it is working. The best conditions for it to pump are as follows: winds need to be light and from the north-east or north, and a good southerly or south-easterly swell with waves from 1 to 2.4 m makes for the best line-up. It is best surfed on a low to low incoming tide and the waves deteriorate rapidly as the reef deepens. The wave itself is a long hollow left-hand reef break that fires off over a shallow, urchin-infested reef. When conditions are right, on a bigger swell with a light offshore, the wave can provide an intense barrel section and a long vertical wall that curves around the bowl to provide an exciting and challenging ride. Surfers coming out here should be paddle fit and confident on fast left-handers.

MIDWAY BEACH

Midway or Waikanae Beach is the town beach for Gisborne city. The beach extends from Turanganui River and the harbour in the north, south through the curve of Poverty Bay to the mouth of the Waipaoa or Big River. There are two camping grounds within 200 m of the bay, a surf club and, along Salisbury Rd, a selection of motels that front the beach.

Waikanae Beach is a gentle sloping golden sand beach that faces south-east. To the north Tuaheni Pt and The Island stop north-easterly swell from getting in, while the southern end is protected by Young Nicks Head. The gentle slope of the beach makes the surfing best on an incoming tide from middle to high. The waves are usually soft and have a tendency to close out on banks that change continuously. The best-sized swell is from 0.6 to 1.5 m and the best direction is south-east or south.

There are two main breaks on the beach, the first being **The Pipe**. It is a right-hand bank that is a few hundred metres south of the Midway Surf Club on Centennial Marine Drive. Pipe is the most consistent surf break on the beach and, by other Gisborne breaks' standards, still reasonably inconsistent. It is best surfed on an incoming tide in swell from 1 to 1.8 m with a north-westerly or westerly offshore. Pipe can be good and has often provided good tube sessions, but the form of waves depends on the sand.

At the southern end of the bay at the end of Centennial Marine Drive is the **Waipaoa River Mouth** or **Big River**. It too is a finicky break, but when it is big and pumping those who have surfed it have likened it to small Nias. It is a hard break to check out from the beach as the white water from waves in the foreground hides the peeling waves out the back. It is a big right and left although few are game to attempt the left. It breaks best in a big southerly swell from 1.8 through to 2.4 and 3 m in light winds from the west. It will break on any swell from the north-east through to south, but the south swells have the power and size that the bar needs. It is a long hot dog wave with plenty of good long tube sections when the sand and gravel bar below is in good form. The bar is a long way offshore, 500 to 800 m off the beach, and the best access to it is out through the river as the paddle around the break will have your arms turned to jelly before you can catch a wave. If the swell is up around the 2.4-m mark, then a slightly longer board will be a great help in catching the waves and making the sections. If you get this place when it is pumping you are in for a great session.

⑨ MAHIA PENINSULA

The Mahia is a large triangular-shaped peninsula that juts out from the East Coast to separate Gisborne's Poverty Bay to the north and Hawke Bay to the south. Mahia is off SH2 about 40 km south of Gisborne and is well signposted. The turn-off is at Nuhaka, where the main highway takes a sharp right-hand turn to continue on to Wairoa.

The peninsula's history saw the Maori tribe Ngati Kahungunu come north to settle here from Napier after suffering at the hands of a number of western tribes who gained the advantage of muskets early during the tribal wars. But after the Pakeha arrived the wars died down and the Maori were able to return to their homelands.

The peninsula today has a large population of Maori farmers and fishermen and the area is rich in sea life. The coasts offer good fishing and diving (when the surf is flat). The town of Morere, just to the north of the Nuhaka turn-off on SH2, offers surfers hot springs to soak out the chill of the cold peninsula waters, a pub to wash down the salt or get a feed fit for a king (and big enough to kill the meanest appetite) and pub, motel, cabin or tent site accommodation.

On the peninsula itself, there are a number of places to stay or camp. The best camping ground to stay at is at Opoutama, in the north-western corner of Opoutama Beach. Blue Bay Motor Camp has a well-stocked shop, excellent and moderately priced cabin accommodation, and acres of good camping ground in the shelter of a forest of mature pine trees. The camping ground has several good breaks within a short walk as well as a post office and garage and is a good base to set out from. To the south-east at the other end of the bay is Mahia Beach, a holiday resort settlement with lots of holiday homes, the second of Mahia's camping grounds, which also has good motel accommodation and a store, and there is a fish and chip shop. The nearest

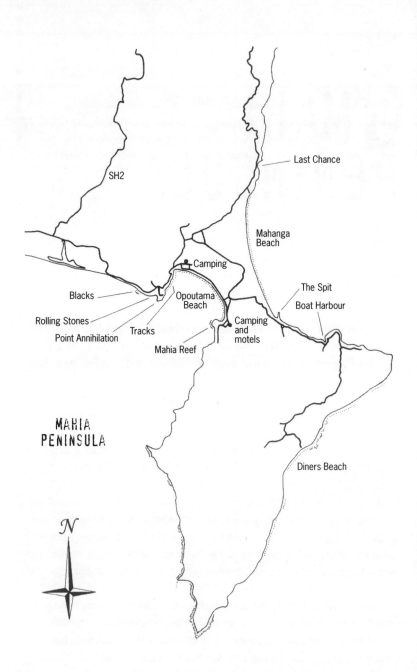

SH2

Last Chance

Mahanga
Beach

Camping

The Spit

Boat Harbour

Blacks

Opoutama
Beach

Rolling Stones

Camping
and
motels

Point Annihilation

Tracks

Mahia Reef

MAHIA
PENINSULA

N

Diners Beach

petrol is either in the town of Mahia further along the Mahia road, at Opoutama or back at Nuhaka.

Mahia Peninsula is one of the east coast's premier surf locations and offers surfers a wide range of different types of waves and breaks that work in swell from all easterly directions, south and even south-west. Mahia has some good barrelling waves and some of the best and most consistent big wave spots on the east coast. There are a number of different breaks on the peninsula, many of which are not listed here. There are reefs all around the northern side that break during north-east, east or big south-east swells, and on the west-facing side of the peninsula that picks up the big southerly swell as well as south-west and south-east swell. If the southerly swell gets too big for the western breaks, then the swell will begin to wrap around and come into the eastern side.

The climate around the Mahia Peninsula can change from one extreme to the other in a matter of minutes. Surfers need always to carry plenty of warm clothing and thick wetsuits when venturing out here in search of waves. Even in the middle of summer, should the weather make a change to southerly, the conditions can rapidly deteriorate to almost subantarctic. In the winter, surfers would do well to remember their thermal underwear and 5-mm wetsuits, gloves and boots. You may not think a Gath helmet looks particularly cool in the water but it will stop the icecream headaches and allow you to stay out in the waves a lot longer.

The breaks are listed in the order in which they lie as you drive out along the peninsula from SH2 at Nuhaka.

BLACKS

Blacks is the first break that you come to on the Mahia road and you will see it not long after the road reaches the coast. There are two carparks that overlook it, one on the corner right in front of it and one further on just before you begin to wind up the hill. Blacks, a reef break, is mainly a right-hander, but it also has a reasonable left. It faces south-south-west and is best surfed in a northerly, north-westerly or north-easterly wind. The wave breaks over boulders and a low weed-covered reef and is best in swell from 1 to 1.8 m from the south-west through to south-east. It is a good and reliable wave that has a fullish take-off followed by a long wall that can offer the odd barrel section on the inside. The wave can break for about 70 m or more through onto the gravel beach. There is also a left-hander that peels off down the other side of the reef and in a south-east swell this too can provide some good waves. The wave is generally quite easy to surf and provides its best form on an incoming tide. On the low tide the reef can get very shallow and the best waves are around mid tide. Blacks almost always has a small wave and even when the wind is a bit dubious you can usually get a surf here.

ROLLING STONES

Rolling Stones is the next wave heading west. As you head inland away from the coast the road goes under a railway bridge. A few metres further on there is a road off to the right that takes you out to the fishing port of Waikokopu. At the end of the road is a carpark that overlooks Opoutama Beach. Stones is a short walk over the hill behind the small village and there is a fence crossing and track to follow.

Rolling Stones is one of the heaviest of the breaks at Mahia. It is a right-hander that breaks over a boulder-strewn bottom down the right-hand side of the cove. This wave is best surfed on a mid to full incoming tide and in a swell from the south. Stones doesn't really start to work until the waves are 1.8 m and it can hold a solid 3-m swell. Entry and exit into the cove can be difficult and this break should only be surfed if you are very confident. Rolling Stones, as you will find out if you go out here at half tide on a 2.4- to 3-m swell, got its name because the huge boulders that you surf over actually can be heard moving as the swell rides up over them and surges up and down the boulders on the shore. This wave is dangerous and very heavy. The take-off is over a ledge that sucks up at the last minute leaving the surfer with a vertical or sometimes over vertical take-off over a huge boil. The wave then races off for about 10 m and some fast thinking can earn the surfer a stand-up barrel. The wave then continues as a steep wall with heavy grinding pocket for another 20 m or so. Surfing here in a big swell requires a bigger board in order to get into the monsters early enough to make full use of the barrel and wall and to have enough control. A strong leg-rope is also a good investment because if you lose your board it will have to negotiate the surging white water over the rocks on the inside. Check your leg-rope for nicks before you go out and if you aren't sure whether you can handle it, don't go out.

POINT ANNIHILATION

Point Annihilation is the next break and can be found to the right and south of the end carpark in Waikokopu. There is a short track into the bay about 30 m from the carpark. Best viewing is from the rocks around the breakwater reef that juts out into the bay inside the break. Best entry points are either north of the breakwater reef in the calm hook, which also makes for an easy exit but quite a long paddle, or into the bay on the inside of the break. The waves are best in a southerly or south-easterly swell with winds from the west. It is best from 1.5 to 2.4 m and can be surfed on all tides. It is a right-hand point break that peels for about 70 m over a combination of boulders and reef. The wave is generally quite heavy, but the ease of entry and exit makes it a good spot to try out some bigger waves. It starts as a fast-section filled wall that rifles off for about 30 m before bowling up and peeling off as a short wall and steep pocket as it curves around the reef into a small boulder bay. When conditions are good the first section can provide good barrels and an exciting and fast-moving wall.

TRACKS

Tracks is the next break and it can be seen from the same carpark as Point Annihilation but back towards Opoutama along the point. The break basically starts just to the south of the boat harbour where the railway tracks follow the edge of the coast — hence the name. The best place to check it out is from the lookout on the hill on the Mahia road heading to Opoutama or from the beach carpark back at Opoutama or the Blue Bay Motor Camp.

Tracks is quite a sheltered break and can be surfed in winds from north-easterly or northerly through to south-westerly. It is a right-hand point break that peels down beside the railway tracks over a combination of reef and sand. It needs a fairly big swell to get in here. When Point Annihilation is 2.4 to 3 m the waves at Tracks are at their best at around the 1.2- to 1.8-m mark. It is best on a mid incoming tide but can be surfed on any tide. The waves vary according to the direction of the swell and the time of the tide but generally offer quite long rides with a variety of different sections. The surfer can take off at any stage of the wave and, apart from on the low tide, the take-offs are usually fairly mellow. The best method of getting out is to walk down the railway tracks (watching out for trains) to the area where the retaining wall has collapsed. Jump into the line-up between the sets, watching out for the shallow reef, and paddle out across the line of the breaking waves. The waves can also be reached by paddling out from the beach, though it is a considerably longer journey than by way of the railway.

OPOUTAMA BEACH

Opoutama Beach stretches 6 km from Tracks to Mahia Beach in the south-east. It is a gentle sloping beach that offers little in the way of good waves. It is best in a small swell from the south-west or south in winds from the north-east. The best wave size is from 0.6 to 1.2 m and the banks often produce a good long-board wave.

MAHIA REEF

Mahia Reef is the reef that surrounds the steep headland at the southern corner of Mahia Beach. It is a left-hander that only works on a big swell. The waves here aren't as good as many of the other breaks that pepper this piece of coast and so it does not see a lot of surfers. It is best in an easterly or south-easterly wind and in a swell from the south that is too big for the reefs at the other end of Opoutama Beach.

Moving now to the eastern side of the peninsula the waves begin north at Mahanga. There are a lot of good waves on the coast from here north through to Young Nicks Head, in fact there are some excellent reef breaks. Access to many of them is difficult, but for the keen tramper/surfer the area can offer a fun trip.

LAST CHANCE

Last Chance is the last easily accessible break to the north and is an excellent left-hand reef break. Access is a little difficult and requires the permission of the local farmer. The road to Mahanga takes you past the beach settlement up the coast to the north. You need only travel a kilometre or so before you come to a left-hand corner where you can glimpse the sea to the right down through a small gully. There is plenty of space around the corner to park the car, but if you want to return and find it in one piece don't just leap over the fence and head down to the break. First go and see the farmer whose house is up the driveway just around the corner and take a few dollars in your pocket as he will more than likely charge you to go over his land.

The break is a left-hand boulder point that breaks for about 60 to 80 m. It is a fun wave that is best from 1.2 to 1.8 m. It is called Last Chance because it picks up so much swell and is far enough north to pick up a south swell as it wraps around the peninsula. It is offshore in north-west to south-westerly winds and the best tide is around full. The wave moves at a good speed down the point and always has a good pocket and long wall to work. Entry is made off the boulder bank that the wave peels down with a short paddle through the breaking waves to get to the shoulder. Getting in requires a little more effort. Let the waves just wash you along the rocks half way down the point and as the surge washes back down, get your footing and beat a hasty retreat.

MAHANGA BEACH

Pukenui Beach or Mahanga Beach is next on the list, although there are a few good little reefs in between. Mahanga is good on the smaller swells from the north-east or east and favours waves around the 0.6- to 1.2-m mark. The beach faces to the east (offshore in north-west through to south-west) and is reasonably protected by the peninsula from south and south-east swells. The banks vary according to the time of year and there is often a good wave or bank in the far northern corner of the beach. It is best on a mid to high incoming tide and is a relatively easy wave compared with the reef waves that make up the majority of the breaks in this area. Access to the beach is either at Mahanga in the north or on the other side of the lagoon at Oraka.

THE SPIT

The Spit is the next break and is easy to spot from the road. As the main road heads south-east after passing through the township of Mahia, it descends a hill to join the coast. The Spit is, as the name suggests, a spit of reef that sticks out from the shore about 100 to 130 m. At low tide it is easily visible as most of the inside of the reef is dry.

The Spit is a filthy left-hander that spits along the reef and can peel and rifle off for over 100 m or more. It is best in a big north-easterly swell and is offshore in a south-westerly. It is best surfed on a swell from 1.2 to 3 m and the waves are broken into two parts when the swell is below 1.8 to 2.4 m. The inside is a slow fullish wave that has a couple of reasonable sections. It is best from mid to high tide. The outer wave is a very fast, very hollow left-hander that barrels off across the shallow reef. It is best surfed at 2.4 to 3 m with a longer surfboard, stronger leg-rope and plenty of guts. It is a classic big wave when the swell is up and features a hairy vertical take-off, followed by an enormous feathering wall with a section about half way that ledges over a very shallow area of the reef to create a good tube. The wave then fills out to wind into the inside. Out the back, getting caught inside often ends in a hair-raising trip over the shallow reef. Not a wave for the faint of heart.

Looking to the south-west down the coast there are a number of unnamed reef breaks that are particularly good in 1- to 1.8-m waves on all lower tides or on the higher tides in bigger swells. They can provide waves of the best quality and are scattered enough that there is never a crowd problem.

BOAT HARBOUR

Boat Harbour is the name of the break that works directly out in front of the boat harbour a little further down the road to the south-east. It is best surfed a couple of hours either side of high in waves from 1 to 1.5 m from a north-easterly or easterly swell. Access is either from the inside paddling across the harbour or, the most common route, from the rocks to the south-east of the break which takes you across the outside of the take-off zone. The wave is a full-on, start-to-finish barrel that rifles off over knee-deep reef. It is fast and the take-off zone is small. You take the drop, that is if you make it, and pull straight up to set your rail for the tube. The best wind is a southerly and the only things to watch out for (apart from the shallow reef) are the double-ups. The wave hits the reef from fairly deep water to throw out a solid lip as the bottom falls out of the wave. It is an exciting wave if you know what you are doing, but if you aren't used to these fast square take-offs or you are not well briefed on the art of free-fall take-offs and tube-riding, then surfing here will be a nightmare for you and for the others in the water around you.

Further south-east of Boat Harbour the road carries on around the coast at Auroa Point. There are a number of unnamed reefs here and to the south-east that can offer reasonable waves and are worth checking out, especially in a north-easterly swell.

DINERS BEACH

Diners Beach is a short drive further down the road and has some good beach breaks, especially on a smaller swell. The beach faces south-east and when all the other breaks around Mahia are too small there is often a good wave to be found here. It is best surfed in a small south-easterly or easterly swell in waves from 0.6 to 1.2 m. The best tide is mid to high incoming and the waves break over a series of sandbars that change and move about with the seasons. The coast around here is also rich in seafood and there is good fishing to be had from the reefs at either end of the bay. The waves are usually quite hollow and the rides are often short but fun.

10 HAWKE'S BAY

South of Mahia Peninsula lies the bight of Hawke Bay, a large indentation in the coastline that cuts inland from Mahia south to Cape Kidnappers. (The region is known as Hawke's Bay.) This area is not well known for its surf, but there is a series of good breaks in the area for those in search of waves. The beaches are steep, much like the beaches of South Canterbury, with coarse gravel sand, and offer little joy to travelling surfers. However, the headlands, rivermouths and reefs offer the surfer powerful waves that gain their power from the steep inshore beach profile that does little to hinder their approach to the shore — waves not unlike those at Mahia.

If you're planning to stay and surf this region for a while then the most central place is the Napier/Hastings area. There are good waves around the Napier/Clive area and also south of Cape Kidnappers. The whole area offers surfing breaks that face in a variety of directions, thus giving the surfer a good choice when the swell is up.

Some of the breaks in the area are prone to a little localism, so if you are intending staying for more than one surf, show some respect for the locals in the water. Giving up a few waves won't hurt; getting heavy with locals will.

Weather conditions in Hawke Bay vary quite radically from summer to winter. Surfing in a spring suit during summer is quite comfortable. However, when the winter throws up a few south swells, a southerly wind and some rain, the surf takes on a bleak antarctic appearance. If you're not seasoned to the chill in the water, then expect a dose of icecream headaches, numb toes and fingers that won't do what they are told. Winter surfing here requires thick steamers, booties and, if you feel the cold, a Gath and gloves won't go astray either.

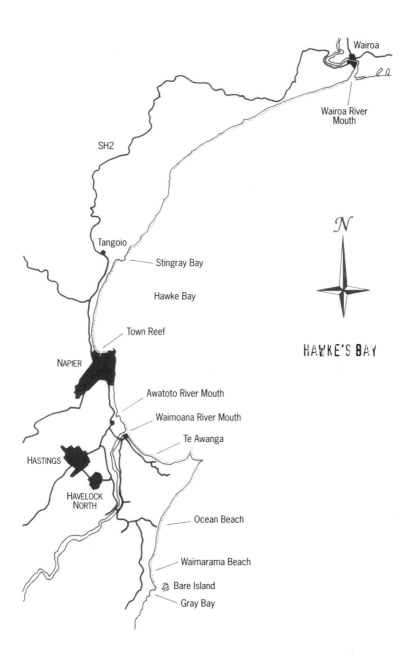

Wairoa

Wairoa River
Mouth

SH2

N

Tangoio

Stingray Bay

Hawke Bay

HAWKE'S BAY

Town Reef

NAPIER

Awatoto River Mouth

Waimoana River Mouth

Te Awanga

HASTINGS

HAVELOCK
NORTH

Ocean Beach

Waimarama Beach

Bare Island

Gray Bay

WAIROA RIVER MOUTH

Wairoa township lies around the half-way mark between Gisborne and Napier on SH2. It has a population of over 5,000 and is the closest town to Mahia Peninsula. The town is well equipped to cater to the traveller, with a good selection of food shops, garages, motels, camping grounds and pubs. The kauri lighthouse that now sits in Wairoa's main street came originally from Portland Island off the southern tip of Mahia Peninsula where it stood from 1877 until it was replaced in 1958. The town is the last stop for many holidaymakers and tourists on their way to Lake Waikaremoana and Urewera National Park.

The rivermouth is 4 or 5 km east of the township and consists of heavy to very heavy hollow shingle-spitting grinders. They are hard breaking over a bottom that feels like coarse sandpaper should you get pitched and dragged over it. The bar is constantly changing and the best time of the year to check it out is from autumn to spring on a good powerful south or south-east swell. The rivermouth faces south-south-east and is offshore in light to moderate north-easterlies. Best size to surf here is in the 1.2- to 2.4-m range on any tide, though on the bigger swell it is best on an incoming tide. Getting to the bar is an easy walk over the beach from the carpark. The hazards to watch out for are the rip from the river, especially if there has been some rain and the river is running high, and the locals who think that they made the break. A little care and a lot of courtesy will get you a few waves and keep you alive. If the surf is no good then try fishing at the rivermouth, there is always a good catch of fresh kahawai waiting in the murky waters.

STINGRAY BAY

Stingray Bay is one of the better surf breaks in Hawke Bay. Access is from SH2 about 25 km north of Napier. Take the Tangoio turn-off and follow the road to the beach. The nearest accommodation is south at the Bay View Motels. There is also a store and petrol at Bay View. Tangoio Beach has a reasonable beach break on a big swell and on a mid to high incoming tide, but the real surf is a few minutes' walk to the north at Stingray Bay. Tangoio also offers good fishing and diving.

To get to Stingray Bay requires a walk north around the rocks from Tangoio.

The bay consists of a right-hand point break that faces east. The wave is best surfed on half to full tide in a 1- to 1.8-m swell. The waves break over a reef and tend to be quite full and soft unless the swell is coming from the north-east, when the wave is a lot hollower and faster. The waves are good for most of the year when there is swell. Winds blow offshore from the north-west to south-west while the best waves are coming from the east or north-east. The rides start outside on the point where they jack up over a ledge to make for an exciting take-off over the shallowest part of the reef, and then bowl along to create a good workable inside section.

If there are no waves in Stingray then take the dive gear; there is plenty of sea life around the reefs and boulders.

NAPIER

Napier is the largest town in Hawke's Bay and has a population of around 50,000. It is a coastal town whose port handles a large percentage of the area's produce and imports. The area was hit by an earthquake back in 1931 that claimed the lives of 256 people; both the cities of Napier and Hastings were virtually levelled. The earthquake also changed the geography of Napier quite dramatically. Prior to the earthquake Bluff Hill was almost an island, in fact it was called Scinde Island. The earthquake raised large areas of the sea floor to greatly broaden the isthmus that joined the hill to the mainland. Rumour has it that before the 'quake there were a number of areas around the hill and harbour that featured good breaking waves.

Napier has plenty of everything for the traveller — accommodation, food, shopping and places of interest. Some of the places that are definitely worth checking out are the Napier Aquarium and the Nocturnal Wildlife Centre. The aquarium was the largest in the country before the completion of Kelly Tarlton's Underwater World in Auckland. It features three floors of tanks that surround a huge main aquarium. The Nocturnal Wildlife Centre is a good place to check out what crawls around our country in the dead of night.

The city is the centre for the many tourists and summer holidaymakers who come to spend a little time in Hawke's Bay and the city is clearly geared up for this trade with prices for dining out, hotel/motel accommodation and souvenirs inflated accordingly. The harbour on the north-western side of Bluff Hill offers yachties safe mooring and on the western side of the harbour's entrance is one of the town's few surf breaks.

The **Town Reef** is the city surf break and is easily accessible through the suburb of Westshore. There is a camping ground in Westshore on the main road and the surf break is right across the road from the Marineland Motel. Heading north from Napier, take the first turn after the bridge that crosses the harbour and then the first left. This will bring you out right in front of the break where there is a carpark, toilets and changing rooms. The wave is not known for its good form but it produces a good workable pocket and wall. It is mainly a right-hander but it does have a reasonable left on some waves. The reef faces north and gets north-east, east or big south swells. The best size to surf here is around the 1.5-m mark, as much smaller and the waves are too slow and soft and any bigger and they close out. It is a good place for learners. Offshore winds blow from the south, but even south-east is ridable here. The best times of the tide are from middle to high, both incoming and outgoing, and getting out is a breeze. You can paddle out from the beach past the remains of the wreck, along the line of the breaking right-hander, or you can go out off the sea wall to the east of the left-hander.

The wave has an easy and fairly flat take-off followed by a workable pocket and a short wall that curves around to follow the reef to the beach. It's best to keep close to the breaking part of the wave, cutting back constantly, though some waves have good sections. The best time of the year to check it out is during the winter when the area gets a lot of big winter south-east swells. The bottom is a flat reef and the best viewing is from the banks in front of the carpark.

The other wave in Napier worth checking out when conditions are right is the **Awatoto River Mouth** about 6 km to the south of the city. Awatoto is the rivermouth for two rivers, the Tutaekuri and the Ngaruroro, and the area is also the centre for a number of Napier's heavy industries, which line SH2 as it follows the coast towards Clive.

Awatoto is a gravel and sandbar that provides an exciting right-hander that can reward the more experienced surfer with some filthy tubes. This hollow rifling right is best between 1 to 1.8 m in an easterly or south-easterly swell. The bar faces east and is an easy walk from the carpark across a paddock to the beach. Awatoto is offshore in west to south-west winds and can be surfed on most tides depending on the shape of the bar. There is no special time of year to surf here — just whenever there is swell. The rip doesn't usually create too many problems and the only things to watch for are the triple-up waves. Negotiating the double-ups is tricky but the barrel that awaits is worth the attempt. But attempting the triple-ups almost always ends in a severe pitching followed by gravel gathering dredging over the bar.

HAUMOANA

Haumoana is a popular resort during the summer months and has all the facilities a travelling surfer could want, except a surf shop. The town has motels, a camping ground and so on, and lies about 10 km north-east of Hastings where there is a surf shop and plenty of pubs. The town lies on the banks of the Tukituki River mouth which offers good kahawai fishing and good whitebaiting during the season.

The **Haumoana River Mouth** is a right-hander at the mouth of the river that breaks over a shallow gravel bar. The wave peels best from 1.2 to 1.8 m in a big south swell or a medium-sized swell from the east or north-east. It is a heavy wave that gets heavier, hollower and faster the bigger the swell gets. The rivermouth faces east and is easily accessible by driving out to its eastern side, north-east of Haumoana township. The state of the waves can easily be checked out from the carpark. The best winds for the bar are south-westerlies and an offshore of 5 to 15 knots can hold up the wave and provide some good barrels. Surfers should always be wary of the rip from the river, especially if the hills have had a bit of rain.

TE AWANGA

Te Awanga is a small town that lies at the mouth of the Maraetotara River in the southern hook of Hawke Bay. It is about 22 km south-east of Napier and 10 km south-east of Clive. This seaside town boasts good fishing and is often used as the stopping and camping spot for travellers heading out to Cape Kidnappers and the gannet sanctuary.

The Maori named the Cape Te Matau-a-Maui, or the fish-hook of Maui — that is, the hook that Maui used to fish up the North Island from the sea. The Cape is world renowned for the gannet colony that nests on the barren slopes some 80 metres above the sea between the months of November and February. The tourist literature boasts of the colony as the only known mainland gannetry in the world but a visit to the easily accessible colony at Maori Bay west of Auckland soon disproves this theory. Four-wheel-drive tours to the colony leave from Napier and Te Awanga to head up through Maraetotara River into the hills and out to the sanctuary. It is a trip worth taking during the nesting season.

Te Awanga has good facilities, camping grounds and cabins and, for those wanting a little more, Haumoana and Clive have all the necessities.

Te Awanga has been surfed for years and offers a good longboard wave most of the year (when the swell is small). It is a right-hand point that breaks over gravel and is easily accessible from the beach carpark. It works best in a north-easterly or easterly swell from 1 to 1.8 m. The right-handers are reasonably soft but with the right winds can provide some hollow sections, especially when the swell is in the region of 1.2 to 1.8 m. The break faces east-north-east, making the offshore wind from the southerly quarter. The best time of the tide varies according to the banks and the best viewing can be had from the area around the carpark.

OCEAN BEACH

Ocean Beach is on the south side of Cape Kidnappers about 15 to 20 minutes' drive south-east of Havelock North. It faces east-south-east and picks up a lot of the southerly and easterly swells. Ocean Beach is a summer holiday resort for many, although there are a number of permanent residents on the coast. If you are travelling here at Christmas, check out the apricots — they are worth stopping off for. Accommodation, petrol and all facilities are available at Havelock North.

Ocean Beach's surf consists of heavy beach breaks most of the time and the bigger the swell the heavier the waves. They are hollow rights and lefts that fire over the steep beach bars. The beach breaks best in a south or south-easterly swell in waves from 1 to 1.8 m. Offshores blow from the westerly quarter and a reasonable offshore turns the most sedate of waves here into hollow thundering barrels. The best winds are light to moderate westerlies. The waves break for most of the year and there is almost always a good bank somewhere up or down the beach. The bottom is mostly sand or sand over rocks and the waves are best surfed from mid to high on an incoming tide. When the swell is small, the beach can provide good waves on most tides. The only hazards to watch for, apart from the rip in a big swell, are the hot locals who have the place pretty well wired.

WAIMARAMA

Waimarama is a small beach resort and farming township about 6 km south of Ocean Beach or 27 km south-east of Havelock North. It is a good surf beach and has a camping ground with cabins available, a garage and a shop. To the south-east, a few hundred metres offshore, lies Bare Island, and the area has good fishing from the beach, south around the coast towards the island and further south to the next bay.

Waimarama Beach has excellent sand and reef breaks in any swell from the north-east through to the south. There is a good left-hand reef break and a series of right and left peaks on the beach that break over a combination of reef and sand. In light to moderate offshores the beach can produce some fast and hollow barrels. The best time to surf here is in a south-east swell from 1 to 1.8 m and a south-west wind. Best time of the tide is on the incoming from mid to high as when the tide starts to go out the beach tends to become messy and close out. If the conditions are looking good then stopping over for a few days here will often provide the travelling surfer with some good waves.

There is another excellent break called **Cray Bay** further to the south over the hill. It has good diving (hence the name) and a hot reef break. The reef is called (according to the spot you take off) **First Left** or **Second Left** and is a very heavy left-hand reef break. The wave is hollow and vertical and best surfed from half to full tide.

When the swell gets over 1.8 m at Waimarama Beach then it is time to hotfoot it over the hill to Cray Bay. The bay faces the south and picks up swell from north-east right through to the south. It can be surfed from 1.2 m and can hold up to a solid 3 m, but the entry and exit in a big swell can prove very difficult. Surfers getting in the water here for the first time would do well to either watch where the locals get in and out or check it out very thoroughly before attempting it. To surf here in a big swell needs a good leg-rope and a sound knowledge of the duck-dive.

The bay is offshore in a north-westerly wind and the only way to check it out is by walking over the hill. The waves break over a shallow rock- and boulder-strewn reef and the wave has a heavy and vertical take-off in the bowl outside. The wave then peels through with a good vertical wall into a fast and often hollow inside section.

Cray Bay, if you get it when it is on, is one of the best waves in the area but watch out for the farmer. If he catches you on his land, he is likely to shoot you.

So a little respect will keep you alive to surf here again, and if you like big heavy waves then I don't doubt that you will want to return.

11 WAIRARAPA /WELLINGTON

The Wairarapa and Wellington areas have a wide variety of surf. While the Wellington beaches are inconsistent and prone to wind swells, the Wairarapa is consistent, often big and always powerful. Wellington is an excellent windsurfing area as opposed to a surfing one, though it does get reasonable waves. But when there are reasonable waves on the Wellington beaches there are always better ones elsewhere.

The Wairarapa, on the east coast, has a steep profile, the water deepening quickly to allow swell to reach the coast without losing too much energy. The result is that some of the country's premier big wave spots are found on this south-east-facing coastline. The Wairarapa coastline is largely inaccessible and it seems that wherever there is access to the coast there are good waves. Some of the access is a little hard on the vehicles but the quality of the surf makes the trip worthwhile.

The coast between the breaks that are mentioned is largely unexplored by surfers, and if you are into hiking for waves a tramp down this coast during the late summer could prove to be very rewarding. There are a couple of good tramps that are well documented that also have good waves. There is a good walk along the coast from the legendary White Rock south to Ning Nong Pt around Cape Palliser. Weather conditions around this coast are unpredictable and can change for the worse very quickly, so be prepared. The worst conditions come with a southerly change, so check the forecast before setting out.

WAIRARAPA/WELLINGTON

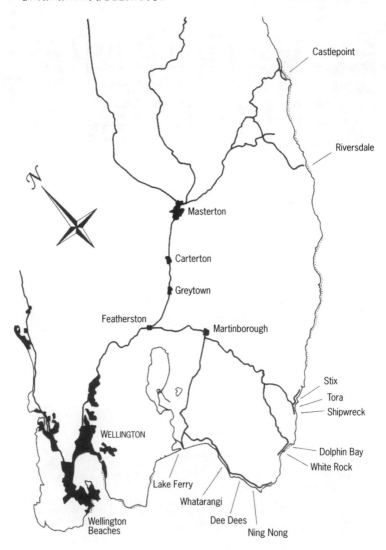

CASTLEPOINT

Castlepoint is a small town about 70 km north-east of Masterton on the east coast. The headland was named by Captain Cook and has a lighthouse and a small port that during the late 1800s was the main shipping outlet for the Wairarapa. The town has camping facilities, cabins, motels and other amenities needed for a stopover as well as good surf. To get to Castlepoint, head out east through Masterton to Te Ore Ore; the road is signposted from there to Castlepoint.

The area has four main surfing spots. The first is **Castlepoint Beach** which is to the right down from the rivermouth towards the point. The beach is good on all tides and most swells except a southerly which has trouble getting in around the point. It is best in winds from the north-west, west or south-west. The waves are heavy beach breaks that stand up on sandbars off the bay to form a series of right and left peaks up and down the beach.

Slippery, or **The Reef**, is a left-hander that breaks on a shallow reef out in front of the rivermouth. It is a powerful wave with a stand-up take-off followed by grinding pocket and vertical wall that peels onto the beach. The Reef is best surfed on a mid to high tide on any swell that has east in it. A southerly, unless it is very big, doesn't get in here. The Reef is offshore in westerly winds and is ridable in waves from 1.2 to 3 m.

South of the beach is **The Gap**, a grovelly little beach break that is surfable in almost all conditions. It is a right-hander that breaks on the beach inside the lagoon. The swell needs to be pretty big for the waves to get in and it is usually only on a high tide that it works. It's a good place for learners.

South of Castlepoint is **Christmas Bay**, a sheltered bay that is good even in a north or north-east sea breeze. The bay can be reached by a short walk straight up and over the hill to the south of The Gap, about a 15-minute hike. There are numerous peaks on a broad sandy beach, all of which can be surfed on any tide and in swell from north-east through to south. The beach is best in waves from 0.6 to 1.8 m.

RIVERSDALE

Riversdale is a small beach resort at the mouth of the Motuwaireka Stream. Access is via the road to Castlepoint, but turn off to Whareama and then onto

Homewood Rd and out to the beach. There are camping facilities there but everything else should be brought with you. The surf is fairly tame as far as the Wairarapa coast goes, but the beach breaks can produce some good tubes and steep walls. The beach is susceptible to rips and water movement in big swells but in smaller waves, from 0.6 to 1.8 m, the sandbars can have some fun rights and lefts. The beach faces east and can be surfed on any tide and in any swell from the north-east through to the south.

TORA

Tora is the first of this area's notorious big wave breaks. Tora is just to the south of the mouth of the Awhea River. Access is through Martinborough, out along White Rock Rd to just past Tuturumuri where Tora Rd intersects on the left. The surf is at the end of the road at the mouth of the Awhea River. To the north is the first of the breaks, called **Stix**. It is mainly a left with a less consistent right as well. It is a reef break that faces the south and is best at low tide. The reef tends to get more swell than the other breaks at Tora and is often good if the Bombora is too small. The reef is offshore in north-westerlies or westerlies.

Tora's main break is **Bombora**, a heavy left-hander that breaks over a shallow reef about 400 m off the beach. The Bombora is directly out in front of the road's end, looking left, and is only surfable at high tide. It is a big wave break that doesn't start to look any good until the swell is over 1.8 m and it is capable of handling up over 3 m. It is offshore in south-westerlies and prefers a south-easterly swell. Inside the Bombora at the rivermouth is a high tide reform that is a good fun wave when everything is out of control.

South of the Bombora is **Tora Point**, a long grinding right-hand point break that peels off over rock shelf and boulders. The point is good in any swell from the east or a very big southerly swell. It is offshore in south-westerlies and can be surfed on any tide. Tora Point works best in a 1.8-m swell but it will still offer good but heavy waves up to and over 3 m.

Shipwreck is a right-hander further south past Tora Point. It is mainly rights with the occasional left on an easterly or north-easterly swell. Shipwreck needs a huge swell to wrap around the long point and get in to the surf break. It is best in a south or south-east swell and in waves from 1.2 to 1.8 m. Offshores are west or south-west and the bay can be ridden on any tide.

WHITE ROCK

White Rock is hailed by many as New Zealand's premier big wave surf location. Surfers coming here should be prepared to deal with a wide range of weather conditions and the heaviest surf on the coast. Access to White Rock is from Martinborough out to the south-east on White Rock Rd. There is accommodation at a deerstalkers' hut a short walk from the road's end. The road is rough going, especially towards the end. As the road heads south around the bay there are a number of small fords to cross that are normally fairly dry. If you are in overnight, watch for rain that can quickly raise the levels of the fords to make them impassable for a few days.

On first arriving at the beach there are two spots to surf. The beach breaks right out in front and, when the swell is small, **Dolphin Bay** is the next bay north and always has waves when everywhere else is flat. But the real surf is south at the end of the road.

The Spit is the long dry reef that extends north-east from the southern end of the bay. It is both a right and a left depending on the angle of the swell. It is best in 1.8- to 2.4-m waves but can be surfed in swell from 1.2 to 3.7 m plus. The Spit works best from half to full tide and in light offshores that blow from the south-west. This is a stand-up barrel wave, both to the right and the left, and the lower the tide the more it sucks. Paddling out can be from either side of the Spit from the inside. Remember when surfing these waves to check your leg-rope for nicks that may cause it to snap.

Seconds is the next break and is on the south-eastern side of the bay south of The Spit. It is a right-hand point that gets as heavy as any waves in New Zealand. It is a grinding wave that peels around a rugged boulder point dragging the surfers caught inside to a nasty end on the steep boulder bank on the inside. It is best on mid to high tide in a south-east or easterly swell or sometimes a huge southerly swell. Easiest access during big swells is by paddling across from The Spit. The deerstalkers' hut is directly above the break on the hill and the wet-back stove can be well stoked up to provide hot showers after a bone-chilling session. The wave is best from 1.8 to 3.7 m and even bigger if the swell is lined up.

LAKE FERRY

Lake Ferry is in the centre of Palliser Bay and can be reached by heading south from Martinborough, through Tuhitarata and on to the Lake Ferry seaside township. It is a popular holiday spot on the shores of the Lake Onoke tidal lagoon. The mouth of Lake Onoke can provide excellent waves when the flow from Lake Wairarapa and the Ruamahanga River is up a little. The Pipeline-type wave is best from mid to high tide on a 1.8- to 2.4-m southerly or south-easterly swell. The wave sucks up shingle, gravel and unsuspecting surfers as it grinds off over the shallow bar. Offshore winds blow from the north to north-west but if the winds are too strong you will not get down the face before the wave pitches you onto the dry bar. When it is on, the waves are hot and it is worth checking out when conditions are looking good.

WHATARANGI

Whatarangi is on the Whatarangi road heading out towards Cape Palliser. It is a Bombora Reef break in front of Whatarangi that is best from low to mid tide. The reef is around 300 m offshore and is best in southerly swells in waves from 1.2 to 2.4 m. Offshores around these parts are fickle things due to the high mountain range that backs onto the surf breaks, but an offshore is north to north-east. Early morning offshores are the best winds to rely on and are the most predictable feature of the weather around the Cape.

At the other end of the bay, heading south-east, is a left-hand point break that is good from 1.8 to 2.4 m. It is a good place to surf when the waves at Ning Nong are huge. It is good in north or north-easterlies but a north-wester comes down the beach and creates a nasty cross-chop.

DEE DEES

Dee Dees is about 4 km south-east of Whatarangi. It is a wave not unlike Meatworks in Kaikoura and breaks on a reef beach. It is best in a big swell from 1.8 to 2.4 m and is predominantly a right-hander with the occasional left as well. The wave is usually a big sluggish fat monster, but it can have some exciting sections. Good for long-drawn-out bottom turns and round-house cutbacks. The coast from here to Cape Palliser is peppered with breaks, and surfers can usually find their own deserted peak on smaller swells.

NING NONG

Ning Nong Pt is a long left-hand point about 1 km from Dee Dees. Recently the point also gained a new name associated with a white ferro toilet that was installed there. **Craps** or Ning Nong can be surfed on all tides but its form depends a lot on the angle of the swell. The boulder reef works best in a clean southerly groundswell in waves from 1.2 to 2.4 m. The offshores are best in the early morning and light winds are required for the best waves.

WELLINGTON

Wellington is not what a surfer would call the hub of New Zealand surfing. It is, at best, inconsistent, and when there are good waves in its south-east-facing beaches there are always better waves to be had not too far away on the Wairarapa. If you are stuck there or looking for an after-work surf there are a number of spots worth checking out.

The bays all require the same conditions to work — that is, a big south swell or south-easterly and winds from the north, north-west or west. The first of the bays in the south-west worth a look is **Island Bay**. It has a right-hand reef that works reasonably well in a big swell and a mid to high tide. **Houton Bay** has a reasonable beach break that can be surfed on most tides. **Lyall Bay** has two spots worth checking out. The beach at the western end sometimes has a ridable bank and at the south end is **Corners** or **The Wall**, which is a bank that forms just off the breakwater and can produce good waves especially in a big southerly ground swell. Corners has a stormwater outflow in front of it and the sand is often better after a prolonged period of rain.

Breaker Bay on the eastern side of the airport has a good right-hand reef that can get quite grunty in a strong south ground swell. It is a bit like Dee Why Pt and surfers need to have their wits about them here and be confident in heavy waves.

KAIKOURA

Kaikoura is a quiet little town nestled on the northern side of the Kaikoura Peninsula. The town has a population of around 2 to 3,000 and was originally a fishing village. The name Kaikoura means to eat crayfish and this coastal area was once the heart of the crayfishing industry. There are plenty of roadside stalls selling crayfish and fresh fish but like most of the country's coast the boom days are over.

Today the town is known internationally for another reason. Kaikoura is now the largest whale watching and dolphin swimming area in the country. You can go and see the resident sperm whales by boat, helicopter or light plane, and there are two dolphin swimming operators who offer tourists the opportunity of a lifetime — to swim with dolphins in the wild. It is an experience well worth the dollars.

The town has all the facilities that are required should you decide to stop over for a few days. There are garages, motels, camping grounds, plenty of backpackers' and a couple of good hotels.

A worthwhile excursion when in Kaikoura is out along the Esplanade to the seal colony at the end of the road. Seals are often a feature of surfing around Kaikoura and are friendly and inquisitive in the water, but they have been known to drop in on surfers in the waves from time to time.

The coast is rich in surf, scenery and seafood, with several of the South Island's best-known breaks within a few minutes of Kaikoura. The coast also has its own localised weather. The Kaikoura mountain range, with its snow-capped peaks, casts long shadows on the coast and creates its own very distinct weather pattern. The cool air blowing off the mountains creates offshores that blow every morning, and during the winter these localised offshores can blow all day, contrary to the prevailing winds. The waters are cold and the coastline rugged, but the excellent surf can make a trip through this part of the country worthwhile. The best time of year to come here for waves is from autumn through to October. The water during this winter period will require a good steamer and often booties to keep away numb toes and maintain the feel of your board. It is not the water so much as the freezing cold shingle and rocks that you must walk across to get to the water. If there is a good offshore blowing then the water will seem pleasant as the mountain air can cut through even a good wetsuit and chill you to the bone.

There are plenty of breaks in the bays and on the reefs that surround the Kaikoura Peninsula. The breaks listed here are only a few of the better known and most consistent waves on this coast.

MANGAMAUNU

Mangamaunu is probably one of the best-known right-hand point breaks in New Zealand and the first of the major Kaikoura breaks to the north. There is no question that this is one of the most scenic spots in the country, the green of the sea set against a steep backdrop of snow-capped mountains. It lies about 20 km north of Kaikoura on the main highway, SH1, which runs right along the curve of the bay out around the point. Surfers need only park the car on the side of the road to get a good view, and cross the railway line to get to the water.

This is a right-hand point wave that peels several hundred metres along a boulder point into a bay. The point works in swell from 1 to 1.8 m from any direction from south through to north-east. However, in a southerly or south-easterly swell the bay can get quite heavy rips, and during a big southerly swell can provide surfers with a continuous battle to stay in position or get out the back from the bay. Mangamaunu is a good all-round wave that can provide surfers with a variety of different sections to negotiate. The point can be surfed on any tide, with the best waves often around middle tide in a north-east or easterly swell. Offshore winds blow from the south-west through to north-west, but a medium to strong north-westerly can make it quite choppy. Getting out is a breeze. You can enter the water at any point along the boulder point, with the easiest entry in the bay where the waves are much smaller than out the back.

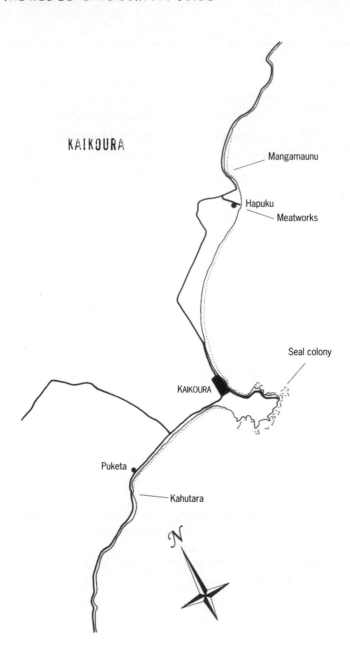

KAIKOURA

Mangamaunu

Hapuku

Meatworks

Seal colony

KAIKOURA

Puketa

Kahutara

MEATWORKS

The next break south towards Kaikoura is Meatworks. The beach is set back off the highway but easily accessible. Take the first right past Hapuku Cemetery heading north towards Mangamaunu. The road will take you across the railway tracks to a boulder beach and you are there.

Meatworks is a series of two or three heavy beach reef breaks that peak up to throw out rights and lefts across the gravel and boulder bottom of the bay. The entry is relatively easy at high tide as the waves break close to shore on the steep profile of the bay. But on the low tide on a big swell it can get a little tricky and surfers should pick their entry point carefully between the sets. The beach breaks better on low tide; on the high tide it tends to get a little full and the waves a bit short if the swell is under 1.5 m. Meatworks will handle swell from 1 to 2.4 m and from any direction from south through to north-east. Offshore winds blow from the south-west to north-west but a south-westerly can chop up the faces of the waves making rides a little bumpy.

KAHUTARA

To the south of Kaikoura is Kahutara, a heavy right-hander that forms at the Kahutara River mouth. The break is about 9 km south of Kaikoura and the turn-off is Puketa. Puketa has a convenient camping ground complete with cabins that are a worthwhile investment in the winter. The rivermouth can handle a swell from 1.2 to 3.7 m and bigger, but the best size to surf here is from 1.8 to 2.4 m on a south swell. The waves peel off over a combination of gravel, boulders and reef, and can provide excellent waves in offshore winds from the west on a low to mid tide.

13 WESTLAND

Westland is probably the most uninviting surfing region in the country, but like all of New Zealand's coastline it too has waves. It is one of the most exposed regions of coast and yet tends to favour smaller swells of 1.8 m or less, but surfers are often unable to surf because the swell is too big or the prevailing westerly winds are blowing. The whole coast gets good waves and if the conditions are right they can be as good as any.

The west coast of the South Island is one of the last frontiers in terms of surfing. It has a very wet climate created by the Southern Alps and the prevailing westerly conditions. Low pressure fronts moving onto the west coast from the South Tasman Sea are stopped by the high snow-capped peaks, forcing the built-up clouds to lighten their loads before rising up and passing over the Alps. During the summer it is quite humid. Moving into the winter the south-westerly airflows can be very cool and the waters icy.

Westport is the first of the towns on the coast heading south. It is a river port situated on the alluvial delta of the Buller River and has a population of around 4,500. The people are friendly and the pubs have a real western atmosphere, with meals big enough to satisfy the hungriest of surfers. The area has two motor camps, a youth hostel and plenty of history relating to the coal trade that has been the backbone of the town since the year dot. Westport has several surf breaks including one freshwater break in the Buller River.

The **Buller Breakwater** often has a good wave in swells from 1 to 1.5 m at half to low tide. It is offshore in a south-easterly to easterly and access is north-west of Westport.

Shingle Beach lies about 800 m inside the mouth of the Buller River and is accessible south across the river out to the mouth. It is best surfed in a north-west storm surf on an incoming tide. The break should be surfed before the floodwaters that follow the storms, as surfing the stormwater coming down the river can confront the surfer with a variety of obstacles from dead cows to sunken trees and debris. The offshores blow from the south-west through to the east.

Tauranga Bay is the first coastal stop after Cape Foulwind on the Cape Foulwind road south of Westport and Carters Beach. The bay has a good left-hand point break at the rocks in the southern end of the bay. It works best in swell from 1.2 to 2.4 m and if the banks are in good form it will hold an even bigger swell. It is best surfed in a west to south-west swell at low tide.

Nine Mile Beach is south of Tauranga Bay on the other side of the left point and is only a short drive south on the same road. The north-western end of the beach offers surfers good left- and right-hand waves on a gently sloping beach. The bay faces the south-west and is offshore in northerlies through to easterly winds.

Punakaiki or **Pancake Rocks** is another good spot to check out. It is best on swell from 0.6 to 1.5 m on mid to high or any tide on a small swell. The coast around the rocks picks up any swell from the north-west through to the south. Punakaiki is a regular stopping place for all the tourist buses and has an excellent camping ground with cabins.

There are waves all along the coast south to Greymouth with good waves at Seventeen Mile Bluff, Fourteen Mile Bluff and Twelve Mile Bluff. The best waves this side of Greymouth can be had at **Nine Mile**.

Nine Mile is a left-hand reef beach break that is best a few hours either side of the tide. SH6 takes you right through the settlement at Nine Mile along the beach. Nine Mile is best on a south-westerly to westerly swell in waves from 1 to 1.8 m. The waves are full of good sections and long workable walls.

Greymouth is the largest of the West Coast towns, with a population of just over 11,000. The town is a river port at the mouth of the Grey River and has a history of gold and coal. Today it is timber which keeps the port operational.

Cobden Beach is the surf beach on the boundary of the suburb of Cobden on the northern side of the Grey River. The banks on the beach come and go and provide mostly lefts that are best surfed on the high tide in swell from 0.6 to 1.8 m. The beach faces south-west and offshore winds are from the north-east to south-east.

Cobden Breakwater is also on the north side of the river and is at the southern end of Cobden Beach. The breakwater has a left and shorter right-hander off a peak just to the north of the wall and will hold a south-west to north-west swell up to 1.8 to 2.1 m. When the swell is bigger getting out becomes a problem that can be overcome on an outgoing tide by paddling out the river. The breakwater is best from half to low tide in winds from the north-west.

On the south side of the Grey River is **Blaketown**, a right-hander off the Blaketown breakwater at the rivermouth. Blaketown is best in a north-westerly to westerly swell from mid to low tide and the form of the waves depends a lot on the shape of the banks. The break is offshore in a north-easterly and is surfable in swell from 1 to 1.8 m.

South of Greymouth there are waves down around the Hokitika area although the swell must be small. South of Hokitika there are waves at Okarito and Gillespies and all the beaches, points and bays in between but, like the rest of the West Coast, they are only surfable if the winds are kind and the swell not too big. South of Haast access to the coast becomes difficult but the waves break all the way to the Sounds. Rumour has it that some of the country's premier big wave locations are on this stretch of coast. But places like Awarua Bay are accessible only by plane, boat or rugged tramp.

14 CHRISTCHURCH

T he Christchurch coastal region extends around both the northern and southern sides of Banks Peninsula and has a few good breaks to offer surfers. The city suburbs sprawl out from the central city to the north-east coastline around New Brighton and Sumner Beach.

NEW BRIGHTON

New Brighton is the north-easternmost suburb of the city and borders the long sandy New Brighton Beach. The area has several motor camps and also boasts Queen Elizabeth II Park, which hosted the 1974 Commonwealth Games. The beach has a gentle sloping golden sand profile that makes for good surf on the many banks that shift around from swell to swell. The best size is from 1 to 1.5 m on a mid to high incoming tide. The surf rolls in to peak up on sandbars up and down the beach, the best swell coming from the north-east or east. However, a big south-easterly swell can swing around Banks Peninsula to break as well. Offshores blow from the west or south-west.

SUMNER

To the south of New Brighton on the south side of the estuary is Sumner. There are two places to surf here — on the bar at the estuary mouth or on the main beach. The bar is best on a low incoming tide on a north-easterly swell and is a left- and right-breaking rivermouth. To the south-east Sumner Beach curves around The Esplanade to a rocky point. The beach is best surfed on a north-easterly, easterly or big south-easterly swell in waves from 1 to 1.8 m. It can be surfed on any tide, the best waves being on mid to high, especially on a bigger swell. The winds blow offshore from westerly to southerly and when the swell is big there is easy entry from the south-east end of the bay at the boat ramp.

TAYLORS MISTAKE

Taylors Mistake is the next break to the south-east out along the peninsula. Taylors is a little cove on the other side of the Sumner Head and is believed to have been named after the bay was mistaken for the entrance to Lyttelton Harbour. Getting there is easy, with Taylors Mistake Rd being well signposted at the south-eastern end of Sumner.

Cut into the steep Port Hills, the bay is probably the best beach break that Christchurch has to offer. It is also the most popular of Christchurch's surfing locations. The profile of the beach is steep and waves break here on all tides. The best swells come from the north-east or east but a big south-easterly swell will also provide waves. Offshore winds blow from north-west through to south-west and the beach can be divided into three main surf breaks. All the waves here peel over steep sandbanks and form good grinding peaks, walls and tubes. The beach can handle waves from 0.6 through to 2.4 m and is best from 1 to 1.8 m. At the south-eastern end of the bay there is a right-hander that peels off the point below the cliffs into the bay. This right-hander is best at low tide. The middle of the beach has good right- and left-hand beach breaks on the steep banks and the form depends a lot on the shape of the bars. At the north-western end of the bay is a left-hander that peaks off the point and again peels into the bay. This left is a little less consistent and requires a good build-up of sand on the point to work.

MAGNET BAY

Magnet Bay is a small indent on the south side of Banks Peninsula. It is around 70 km south of Christchurch and is reached via Halswell Rd and SH75 out past Lake Ellesmere to Birdlings Flat where the surf can be checked before continuing on inland around Lake Forsyth. The road meanders down through some rugged Banks Peninsula scenery, past Te Oka Bay, which also has

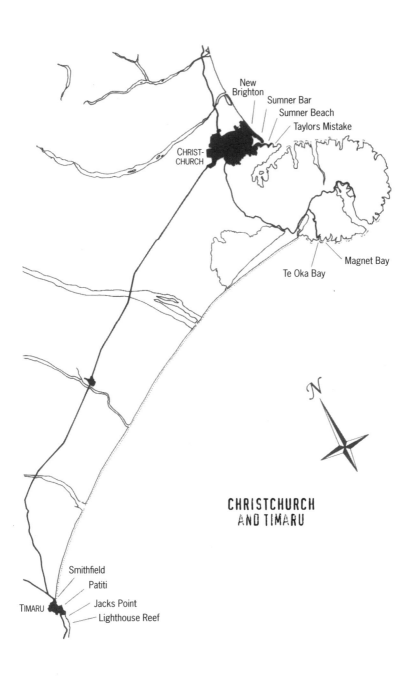

New
Brighton
Sumner Bar
Sumner Beach
Taylors Mistake

CHRIST-
CHURCH

Magnet Bay
Te Oka Bay

N

CHRISTCHURCH
AND TIMARU

Smithfield
Patiti
Jacks Point
TIMARU
Lighthouse Reef

reasonable waves, and sharp left to Magnet Bay. The last stretch of the road is pretty heavy going and all care should be taken.

Magnet Bay has been surfed since the early sixties when it was discovered as a surfing location by members of Christchurch's Midshore Boardriders Club. Magnet isn't really a bay at all, but consists of a boulder and bull-kelp-covered left-hand point that leads into a shallow kelpy cove. It faces pretty well due south and accordingly receives south or south-east swells that power in from the southern depths without having to refract around any land. The result is powerful left-hand waves that push down a shallow boulder reef. Offshore winds blow from the north-east to hold up waves from 1.2 to 3 m, to produce a fast hollow wave that is best ridden from half to full tide. Watch entries and exits through the forest of bull kelp that can easily entangle and drown a surfer. The barnacle-encrusted rocks, too, can be nasty if you're not careful. Entry is best from the point across and into the bay. Magnet Bay is undoubtedly the best break in the Christchurch area and gets all the southern swells that Taylors Mistake and other beaches on the northern side of Banks Peninsula miss out on.

15 TIMARU

The city of Timaru lies at the southern end of the Canterbury Bight 160 km south of Christchurch and 200 km north of Dunedin. The city has a deepwater port protected by a series of concrete breakwaters and all the facilities a travelling surfer could need, including pubs, motels, camping grounds, shops and waves. There is a camping ground at either end of the city. The Selwyn Holiday Park in Selwyn St to the north has good camping and cabin accommodation. The city has a population of about 40,000 and only a few of the hardcore surfers around the coast are human — the others are either seals or eaters of seals. The waves of Timaru are hardcore, most of the breaks pitching out further than they are high. The beaches around this area of coast are almost all shingle from the many river deltas that pepper the coast.

The weather down here gets pretty cold, the southern storms of winter freezing the rain on the car windscreen as it hits. Your spring suit becomes obsolete this far south unless you are acclimatised to the chill of the water and southern winds so bring a good wetsuit, booties and maybe even gloves and a Gath.

SMITHFIELD

The first break in the north is Smithfield, which barrels directly out in front of the Smithfield Freezing Works a few kilometres north of the city centre. A signposted road takes you out across the railway tracks to the beach in front of the freezing works. This surf spot is definitely not for the faint-hearted. Local surfers believe this break to be the nearest thing New Zealand has to Australia's Shark Island. It is an extremely heavy right-hand reef break that pitches out further than the face of the wave is high. Surfers need only bring their guns to surf here and it can only be surfed a half hour to an hour either side of high tide. Its power reflects the origins of the southerly swells that it works on and the offshore winds blow from the west. Smithfield breaks best from 1.8 to 3 m and can handle a bigger swell if the conditions are right. Surfers would do well to remember that the waves are within spitting distance of the freezing works and the break's comparison with Shark Island runs deeper than just waves. This area from Timaru south to Dunedin is white shark country, so watch your toes.

PATITI

The next break is Patiti, which can be reached through Timaru city. Take the hospital turn-off and follow the road out under the railway to Patiti Beach. The point at the south end of the bay is Patiti Pt. It is a left-hander that breaks over reef down the point and is the most consistent, and consistently surfed, break in Timaru. It works on most swells from north-east through to south and is offshore in winds from north-west to west. Patiti is best on a lowish tide but can provide reasonable waves on most tides.

JACKS POINT

South, the next break is Jacks Point. Jacks is about 3 km south of Timaru via SH1. Turn off at Scarborough Rd and follow it to the beach. The break is a high tide reef that peaks up to form a right- and left-hander. It works best in a north-east or an easterly swell and gets a little shallow as the tide drops. The best winds for the surf here are west and best swell size is around 1.2 to 1.8 m.

LIGHTHOUSE REEF

Lighthouse Reef lies about 200 m south of Jacks and is easily reached by a short walk from where you park the car at Jacks. The reef is another Shark Island lookalike, though to a lesser extent than Smithfield. It is mainly a right-hander but it also has a good left on a south or south-east swell. The waves break at a place called Tuhawaiki Pt (formerly known as Jacks Pt and renamed after the chief of the Ngai Tahu, Hone Tuhawaiki, who drowned here in 1844) and barrel off over a shallow reef. Lighthouse will work in any swell from 1.2 to 2.4 m from the north-east through to south. It is a heavy reef break that pitches out 1.8 m in a 1.8-m swell. The best tide is from half to high and offshores blow from the north-west through to west. If you are a little rusty on your late take-offs or barrel riding, don't bother going out and getting in the way.

16 DUNEDIN

Dunedin is the second largest city in the South Island. The population of around 100,000 live in a city that has the atmosphere of a 19th-century Scottish town. The city rolls across the hills (painted white with the winter snows) down to the south where it is bordered by beautiful sandy beaches and, in the east, by the Otago Peninsula. The heart of the city is made of stone — the churches, the railway station, the law courts and other buildings remind visitors of the people who first settled here from Scotland.

But the Dunedin area was well populated before colonisation, and the early 1800s saw some of the bloodiest episodes in New Zealand's history. Early sealers intent on butchering the local seal colonies then turned their attention to the local Maori. This conflict, the long feud between the local tribes in the late 1700s and the diseases brought by the settlers and sealers drastically reduced the Maori population by the mid-1800s to a mere shadow of the proud and once considerable populations that had lived in the area.

For surfers, the city is a surfing paradise. The waters are cold and during the winter the winds are cutting, but the quality of the surf on this stretch of coast and further south makes it one of the best surfing areas in the South Island. There are beaches on and around the Otago Peninsula that can handle swell from any angle and most sizes, but the key to getting a good surf is checking out the conditions and knowing exactly where to go.

Dunedin also has a reputation, kept in mind by surfers, as the location of most of the country's documented shark attacks. The coast is affected by a warm current that flows close to the peninsula from the north. It is this current that brings the Great White Sharks to the coast in search of their favourite food, seals. The area's seal colonies are once again expanding after their virtual elimination by sealers in the 1800s. Surfers are an easy mistake for

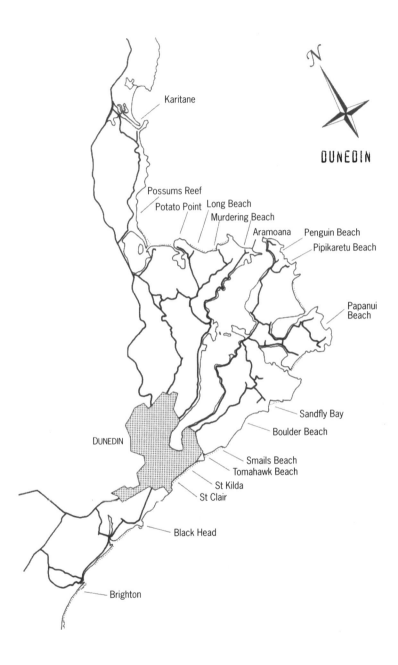

Karitane

N

DUNEDIN

Possums Reef
Potato Point Long Beach
Murdering Beach
Aramoana Penguin Beach
Pipikaretu Beach

Papanui
Beach

Sandfly Bay
Boulder Beach

DUNEDIN

Smails Beach
Tomahawk Beach
St Kilda
St Clair

Black Head

Brighton

sharks to make — in the water in a dark wetsuit the surfer is the same colour and shape as our furry friends. During the summer months, the main town beach, St Clair, is the only place in the country to have shark nets in the water. Watch your toes.

KARITANE

North of Dunedin about 34 km is the seaside resort of Karitane and a break known to surfers as Karitane or **Pipeline**. The breaks are at the mouth of the Waikouaiti River and are easily accessible from the south side. The town has much historical interest. It is where the Karitane Nurses (now a feature of communities throughout New Zealand, providing help for mothers and their babies) first began operating under the leadership of Sir Frederick Truby King.

The rivermouth has two waves — a river bar break called Pipeline that is best in waves from 0.6 to 1.8 m, and a right-hand point that breaks from 1.8 m and will handle any size that the ocean can throw at it. They both face the north-east and are offshore in winds from the south-west, with the point also ridable in a westerly. This spot is only worth it if the swell is big and can close out if the swell has too much north in it. The river bar is best on the low tide while the point is best on the high tide. Getting out is easy through the river, but the point wave is not one for beginners. The wave is very heavy and is Dunedin's big wave spot. It has strong rips on big swells and the point is littered with big rocks covered in entangling bull kelp. It is definitely not a wave for short surfboards or inexperienced surfers. It is a hardcore top-to-bottom wave with exciting, mind-blowing take-offs.

POSSUMS REEF

There are several breaks south of Karitane before Blueskin Bay and the start of the Otago Peninsula. The main break is a reef break about 2 km north of Warrington on the northern side of Blueskin Bay and is called Possums Reef. The spot is a little hard to get to without a local guide and surfers have to cross a private farm to get there. Ask the farmer first. The wave is a heavy duty left-hand reef break that works best on a high tide, an east swell and a west wind. Again, it is not a wave for beginners and when it is 1.8 m plus is for the experienced only.

POTATO POINT

South of Possums Reef the Otago Peninsula begins. The peninsula is divided into two halves by the Otago Harbour which extends to the city, almost to St Clair Beach. On the west side of the peninsula the breaks begin at Potato Point. This is a right-hand point that is not unlike Murdering Bay but is more sheltered by the peninsula and thus receives smaller swells. The road is good and access is by heading towards Long Beach or Purakanui. The point is ridable in winds from the south-east to south and is best in a north-east swell on a low incoming tide.

East of Potato is **Long Beach** which has good beach breaks on the high tide at its western end. It is best in small north-east swells from 0.6 to 1.5 m and is offshore in winds from the south or south-west.

MURDERING BEACH

Murdering Beach or Murderers is one of the best breaks in Dunedin when conditions are right. Access is from Port Chalmers and the port is also the centre for the nearest accommodation, petrol and supplies. The town also has six pubs — more pubs per head of population than Las Vegas! Port Chalmers is the port for the Otago area as well as Dunedin. It also serves as the centre for the commercial fishing industry in the area.

To reach Murderers, head north from Chalmers towards Purakanui and on to Heywood Point Rd. Follow the signposts to the steep access road down into the bay. The road washes out in the wet so be careful driving down. If it is wet, leave your car at the farmer's gate and walk down.

Murdering Beach got its name after the bloody slaughter of some 70 local Maori by the crew of the *Sophia*, a seal boat. While trading with the locals, a Maori recognised one of the sealers as a trader in preserved Maori heads and set upon the party, killing three of them. The ruthless Captain James Kelly then retaliated by attacking another trading party of Maori, butchering them with sealing knives.

Murderers is also home to an excellent right-hand point break at the north-eastern end of the bay. The form of the bay depends on the shape of the sand on the point and it can sometimes get very hollow. The point can be surfed in waves from 0.6 through to 3 m plus but is best around 1 to 1.2 m. The bay faces north and the best waves come from a north-east ground swell; cyclones are the best. The best winds are southerly and the bay is ridable in winds from south-east through to south-west, providing the south-westers aren't too strong. The waves are divided into two parts, with the outside best on the high tide during large swells and the inside best on the low tide.

The wave itself starts with a wicked ledging take-off followed by a long walling ride through to the inside, complete with good barrel sections if the sand is good. The wave is an excellent malibu board wave in small swells. The wave breaks over boulders and reef out on the point and a sand and rock combination through to the sandy bay. Getting out can be difficult on a big swell as the current gets pretty strong. Sometimes a walk out along the rocky point to paddle out across the breaking waves is necessary.

There are several things to be wary of out here. The first is that the driver of the car doesn't get too preoccupied with checking out the surf on the way down the road and drive over the edge. Secondly, when the swell is big the point can get quite rippy and is therefore not recommended for beginners. Thirdly, watch out for sharks. There have been numerous and regular sightings of Great White Noahs out here.

ARAMOANA

Aramoana is known to surfers by many names, including **Aramoana Spit**, **The Spit** and **The Mole**. It is a sandy beach at the mouth of the Otago Harbour. It is an easy and straightforward drive from Port Chalmers along the harbourside Aramoana Rd. The beach is separated from the harbour entrance by a breakwater called The Mole. This breakwater extends for hundreds of metres offshore and the best surf is found beside it. The Mole also acts as an easy entry point to the surf in most sizes of swell.

There are lots of other things to do around this area. The high sand dunes offer good sand surfing and there is good fishing too. The beach faces north and the best winds for surfing here are from the south-west. The best swell is a peaky north-easterly and the beach is surfable in swell from 0.6 to 2.4 m. The beach is excellent on a big clean swell, but getting out can be difficult.

The waves are fast, and the very hollow beach breaks have earned the spot the nickname Tube City. The place works best on mid to high incoming tide and is best in glassy or light offshore conditions. Aramoana also gets the swell better than the other north-facing beaches, and it is often 0.3 to 0.6 m bigger there than at Murdering Beach. The waves are good for most levels of surfing when the swell is small, but once it gets over 1.8 m, a surfer needs to be well versed in the art of duck-diving.

The beach is also notorious for shark sightings, and being so close to the harbour entrance doesn't help. Surfers would do well to keep alert should people on the beach start waving their arms and shouting 'Jaws'.

NORTH-EAST OTAGO PENINSULA

From the Aramoana Spit, the next breaks to the east are those on the north-facing beaches on the eastern side of the Otago Harbour. To get there head out of Dunedin to the south, around the bottom of the harbour and up to Portobello. From there Portobello Rd heads towards the albatross colony at Taiaroa Head. A road just to the south of the point takes you to within walking distance of the first bay, **Penguin Beach**.

All these beaches face north-east or east and are best in waves from 0.6 to 1.8 m. They break best in swell from a peaky north-easterly through to a heavy southerly that wraps around Cape Saunders to get in. The bays are usually calmer than those on the western side of the harbour because the hills protect them from the strong north-westerlies, westerlies and south-westerlies that come down from the mountains. They break on most tides but prefer an incoming to high on bigger swells. The corners of the bays usually offer the best waves with combination reef and sand points.

These bays are sharky because of the many seal colonies scattered around the peninsula. Remember that many of the bays and all of their inhabitants are protected. In those which are wildlife sanctuaries, the seals and penguins have the right-of-way in the waves. Strictly no dogs allowed, for the protection of the wildlife.

South of Penguin Beach and accessible through Pipikaretu Rd is **Pipikaretu Beach**. It often has good sand at the south-eastern corner, and good hollow right-handers can be found there in an east or south-east swell.

Papanui Beach is another beautiful, scenic and isolated surf beach. To get there, follow the signposts or your map towards Cape Saunders. Near its end, Kaimata Rd branches off to the left to take you to within a short walk of the beach. The waves here are good and crowds are never a problem. There is a wreck at the southern end of the bay and good waves at both southern and northern ends.

SOUTH OTAGO PENINSULA

There are a number of good beach breaks and point breaks on the beaches that face south on the southern end of the peninsula. They may be reached via various access roads off Highcliff Rd.

The northernmost of these beaches is **Sandfly Bay** which is off Sealpoint Rd. **Boulder Beach** is accessible by walking track from Braidwood Rd, which is off Sealpoint. At the southern end of the peninsula, just a short drive out of the suburbs, are **Smails Beach** and **Tomahawk Beach**.

All of these bays are best during the summer in small southerly swells. Offshore winds are northerly or north-east and the waves break best from 0.6 to 1.8 m. The beaches are steep and heavy beach breaks that can get quite hollow. The best spots are in the corners of the beaches where the waves wedge up to form good right and left peaks. The best time of the tide depends a lot on the banks, but more often than not it is best on a low incoming tide. The waves get super heavy on a big south swell and the rips can be very strong.

ST CLAIR

St Clair is the main town beach for Dunedin. Its northern end, although part of St Clair, is called **St Kilda**. St Clair is *the* centre of Dunedin for both surfers and the younger generation. It is a good place to check out the surf and just generally hang out. But there are usually better waves to be had on nearby beaches.

The southern end of the beach features a hot saltwater pool on the rocks at the point and during the summer the beach is supposedly protected from sharks by shark nets. There are surf clubs at St Clair and St Kilda.

The beach usually has good sandbanks that can produce powerful beach breaks and deep tubes. It is surfable in waves from 0.6 to 1.8 m, is best on a low incoming tide and is offshore in winds from the north-west. The beach is consistent on all swells but for the point to work it needs a higher tide, westerly winds and a lined-up south swell. The point can get very sucky and quite hollow on small swells, breaking over reef, bull kelp and sand, while the shore break in the corner sucks dry over sand to dump unwary surfers onto the beach. The bigger swells can be made from the channel in front of the pool.

Beware the Great White Munchies, the rips in big swells, the crowds in summer and the icecream headaches in winter.

BLACKHEAD

Blackhead is a good beach break just south of St Clair. It is best in small peaky east swells but is ridable on any swell that gets in and in waves from 0.6 to 1.5 m. The banks vary from swell to swell; the best time of the tide is often at low. The waves are fast and hollow and are reasonably powerful for their size. The bay has a tendency to get quite rippy in swell over 1.2 to 1.5 m and is best surfed on small 1- to 1.2-m easterly swells.

The walking track through to Tunnel Beach is worth a look. It was originally cut in the 1870s to give the Cargill family access to the secluded beach. Also check out the rock columns behind the headland at Blackhead, but watch for falling debris.

BRIGHTON

Oceanview has a good beach break while Brighton has a good right-hand point break. The point is best in a small lined-up south swell at low tide. The best winds are westerly or light south-westerlies. It is a rugged rocky point that, depending on the swell, can offer all levels of ability a fun wave. Getting out is either off the beach or out between the rocks on the point. The wave is best from 1 to 1.8 m and is a good right-hander that has a good workable pocket. It breaks over bull-kelp-covered boulders, and on a small swell the floating kelp can often bring the surfer to a sudden stop. Watch for the dry sections over rocks as the wave bends into the inside.

17. INVERCARGILL AND THE CATLINS

nvercargill is the south of the south, the bottom of the country and home of the country's longest days, nicest oysters and coldest waters. Surfing here is a sport for the very keen and, during the winter months, the very mad. If the icy waters and the instant icecream headaches don't get you then trying to get the wax onto your board will. The city of Invercargill has a population of around 50,000 and the next stop south is Stewart Island, which incidentally has great waves too. The town has several major industries, including the Tiwai Pt Aluminium Smelter, the meatworks and, of course, Bluff oysters.

The people of the area are very friendly and — most unusual — the surfers are almost always glad of company in the waves. Apart from the weather the area has some insane surf breaks, beginning in the Catlins on the south-eastern coast. The Catlins is probably the most unexplored piece of accessible coast in the country and home for some very hot breaks. State Highway 92 is the coastal road that takes the surfer through the Catlins State Forest Park and up the coast to the town of Owaka, a good base for a little exploration in search of waves. The town has a couple of motor camps and all the facilities a travelling surfer could want. The local pubs in this part of the country also serve the biggest meals.

The whole coast from the mouth of the Clutha River south to the Bluff is a virtual surfer's paradise of uncharted and unsurfed beach breaks, reef and point breaks.

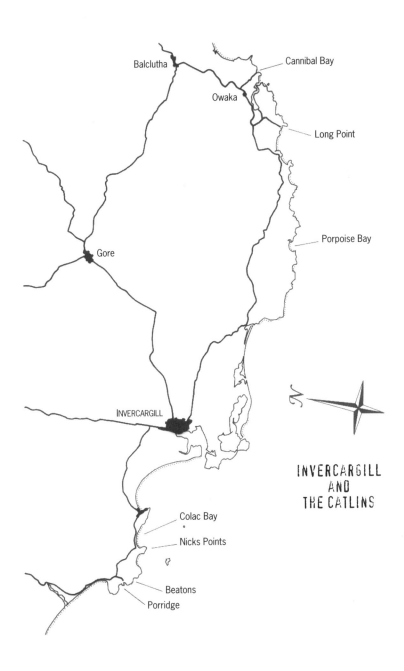

Balclutha

Cannibal Bay

Owaka

Long Point

Porpoise Bay

Gore

INVERCARGILL

INVERCARGILL
AND
THE CATLINS

Colac Bay

Nicks Points

Beatons

Porridge

CANNIBAL BAY

Cannibal Bay is a good beach break in any swell. The beach got its name after a bloody battle between two Maori groups back in the 1830s. Knowing the Maori were cannibals, settlers who found human bones in the remains of a Maori feast dubbed the bay Cannibal Bay.

The surf here is mainly beach breaks, but with the power of the south swells the waves are very heavy and often very hollow on an incoming to high tide. The bay will handle up to 2.4 m, but getting out in a big swell can be difficult. Cannibal faces the south-east and receives swell from the east through to the south. Getting there is relatively easy — the road is signposted on SH92 a few kilometres north of Owaka.

LONG POINT

Long Point is one of the South Island's premier left-hand point breaks and is situated just south of Owaka. Take the turn-off to Ratanui and then on towards Tarara. About half way the Long Point road branches off towards the coast. Long Point is a heavy left-hander that breaks over reef and bull kelp. It can be surfed in waves from 1.2 to 3 m in swell from the east through to the south. It is best on a low incoming tide and in winds from the north-west. The wave is a solid and long left that has a long vertical wall. It is a great hot dog, top-to-bottom wave that has an exciting ledging take-off. It is best from 1.8 to 2.4 m in clean south ground swell.

PORPOISE BAY

The coast from Owaka south to Porpoise Bay is a wealth of breaks and bays and is relatively untouched surfing coast. Access to many of the breaks requires a good walk.

The next spot, and one of the better known surf breaks for Southlanders, is Porpoise Bay. It is a good beach break with a point at the southern end and a harbour mouth and bar at the northern end. The bay is a wealth of breaks in swell from the east through to the south. The southern ground swells offer the best conditions for the southern end of the bay while the bar requires an easterly or south-easterly swell to line up. The bay can handle swell from 0.6 to 2.4 m plus and needs an offshore from the west. The southern end is sheltered in winds from the south-west and even south while the north needs a west or north-west wind to be offshore. Porpoise Bay, because of the variety of conditions it works in and the variety of waves and swells that it breaks on, offers surfers a good all-round spot for a stopover. There is a camping ground in Waikawa, and the surrounding forest has some interesting tramping as well as good trout fishing.

COLAC BAY

South-west of Riverton, which is west of Invercargill on the south coast, is Colac Bay. The bay is just off SH99 at Colac and faces south-east. It is offshore in a north-westerly or westerly and has some good beach breaks in a south swell from 1.2 to 2.4 m.

From here around the coast to Te Waewae Bay there is a concentration of surf breaks on a rocky series of bays and points — places like **Nicks Point** and **Beatons** and the best of the Invercargill breaks, Porridge.

PORRIDGE

Porridge can be found on the coast to the west of Invercargill. Take SH6 north out of Invercargill and turn off onto SH99 at Lorneville. Porridge is about 60 km west, down through the township of Pahia to the road's end. The road ends only 200 m from the break which is over the hill. Go through the farm on the right but be sure to ask the farmer for permission, especially during lambing.

Porridge is a left-hand point break that faces south, thus receiving all the big south swells, and these waves can really pack a punch. Offshore winds blow from the north-east to north-west. Porridge works on any tide but is best on high, and swell from 1.2 to 3 m will peel methodically over the reef and boulder bottom every time. The wave is a fast and hollow left that fires along a shallow rocky shelf, so watch your head if you're nailed. Entry can be made from the lagoon on the inside, out through the gap and into the line-up. It can be tricky getting out through the gap in a big swell but a few good duck-dives will get the more experienced surfers out the back fairly easily. Best viewing is from the bank directly in front of the breaking waves. The break can't be seen from the road, so a 200-m walk is essential. Porridge can be surfed any time of the year providing the pack ice has broken up. This break is as cold as New Zealand's surfing gets, so wear plenty of rubber.

INDEX

Mike Bhana was born in Hamilton in 1963, and developed an early enthusiasm for the more adventurous outdoor activities. As a keen surfer for over twenty years, he researched *The New Zealand Surfing Guide* while chasing this country's best waves, and has also spent several winters pursuing the sport in Australia and Hawaii.

He has been associate editor of *Adventure Magazine*, and editor of both *New Zealand Skier* and *New Zealand Surfing Magazine*. In addition, he launched and edited *New Zealand Windsurfer*.

Mike has developed an exciting career as a photojournalist and, more recently, as a cameraman, specialising in underwater sequences. In 1991, he established Wild Film and Television, and has since produced and directed over 40 programmes for TV3 Sports and TVNZ Sports, and more than 50 television commercials. Since 1993 he has produced three natural history documentaries for *The World Around Us*.